Eheda

GLAMORGAN AVIATION

Eheda

GLAMORGAN AVIATION

Robert C. Thursby

TEMPUS

First published 2002

PUBLISHED IN THE UNITED KINGDOM BY:
Tempus Publishing Ltd
The Mill, Brimscombe Port
Stroud, Gloucestershire GL5 2QG

PUBLISHED IN THE UNITED STATES OF AMERICA BY:
Tempus Publishing Inc.
2 Cumberland Street
Charleston, SC 29401

British Library Cataloguing in Publication Data.
A catalogue record for this book is available from the British Library.

ISBN 0 7524 2752 0

Typesetting and origination by Tempus Publishing.
Printed in Great Britain by Midway Colour Print, Wiltshire

Contents

Acknowledgements

When I first began this work over twenty years ago, I resolved to acknowledge all those who had in some way helped me to accumulate the bank of information which is the substance of this volume. However, with the passage of time their names have become legion and would now fill several pages. So to all those kind people who took the time and trouble to direct, and sometimes to take, a total stranger to 'the place where it happened' or who courteously responded to unsolicited letters and telephone calls as well as old friends and others who have become new friends, I extend my grateful thanks. I also wish to express my gratitude for the assistance and courtesy extended to me by the professional and voluntary officials of the following organisations: The National Library of Scotland, Edinburgh; the Mitchell Library, Glasgow; the public libraries of Birmingham, Manchester, Mansfield, Solihull, Newbury and Worcester; the British Library, London; the British Newspaper Library, Colindale; the Public Records Office, Kew; the Imperial War Museum, London; the National Railway Museum, York; the General Register Office, London; the Royal Aeronautical Society, London; Mr D.F. Burchmore of the Airship Heritage Trust; Old Warden and Mr John Baker of the British Balloon Museum and Library.

Here in Wales: The National Library of Wales, Aberystwyth; Cardiff Central Library; and the public libraries of Barry, Bridgend, Caerphilly, Merthyr Tydfil, Neath, Penarth, Pontypridd and Swansea; the National Museums and Galleries of Wales, Cardiff; Porthcawl Museum; and the Glamorgan Records Office.

Special thanks are due to Ennis Matthews who read the original manuscript and made helpful suggestions; Chris Ware who did the same and also brought his professional skills to bear on some of the illustrations; Mike Woodward of Terence Soames (Cardiff) who breathed new life into some very old photographs; Ken Wakefield for allowing me access to his photographic collection; Molly Sedgwick, distributor of the book *When the 'Chute Went Up* by Dolly Shepherd, for permission to use photographs contained therein; and Gill Sewell who reached the verge of a nervous breakdown transcribing my handwriting into print.

R.C. Thursby
Barry 2002

Introduction

The word *Eheda*, the title of this work, is the imperative form of the Welsh word *ehedeg*, to fly, meaning 'fly forth', which was adopted as the motto of the Cardiff Aeroplane Club in the 1930s.

This book, covering the first 137 years of manned flight in the County of Glamorgan – from the reign of George III to that of George VI – is the result of over twenty years of painstaking research. A list of libraries and other sources of information either visited or consulted is included in the list of acknowledgements, but it might interest the reader to know that I have also visited every site in the county mentioned in the text in person.

The book is aimed at a dual readership: flying enthusiasts, both from Glamorgan and elsewhere with an interest in past events in the county, and others whose interest leans more towards local history in general, who nevertheless might like to know what part aviation had to play and what aerial events took place, in some case literally on their own doorsteps. For the benefit of the latter, usually at the beginning of each chapter, sufficient technical information to render the text understandable has been included. I hope that the former will forgive me for stating, what is to them, the obvious.

All of the information has been obtained from contemporary archives with the exception of some of the background information and the occasional eye witness account. As a result some common myths that have been perpetuated for decades have been exploded as much to the author's surprise as to anybody else's.

In order to place local events in context some reference to aviation history in the wider world has been included in the text, as has a small amount of social and economic history, in order to capture the atmosphere of the times.

I make no apology for the quality of some of the older photographs: they are simply the best available. I have made every effort to credit all illustrations to their correct sources. However, there are a number whose origins are obscure. If I have inadvertently given anybody cause to feel aggrieved I can but apologise.

A Note on Money

Anybody who has worked or played in the aviation world knows only too well that flying and finance are very close bedfellows.

Unfortunately the British monetary system has changed drastically both structurally and in terms of value since the period described in this volume. For the benefit of younger readers, which includes most people under the age of forty, a brief description of the monetary system prior to decimalisation may be of assistance. Under the old system the pound was divided into 20 shillings (the equivalent of the current 5p) indicated by the symbol *s*. Each shilling was divided into 12 pence, symbol *d*, and pennies were divided into halfpennies and farthings, ½*d* and ¼*d*.

The other major factor to consider is the change in the value of money brought about by inflation. Inflation is nearly always with us to some extent but during the twentieth century the British currency underwent three periods of what is sometimes referred to as galloping inflation. They were the periods following the two World Wars and also a period during the 1960s and 1970s. As a result the value of the pound has changed beyond recognition. The problem is further compounded by the change in the value of goods and services relative to each other.

However, a reasonably accurate rule of thumb is as follows: prior to 1914 multiply the value of the pound by 100. Between the wars multiply by 50.

1
Early Days

From their earliest days people have watched the birds and dreamed of flight. It was a dream that took them a surprisingly long time to realize, considering that both the materials and knowledge utilised in the construction of the first successful aircraft had been at their disposal for centuries prior to the event – namely paper and Archimedes' Principle. Put into an aeronautical context, Archimedes Principle states that if a gas that is lighter than the surrounding air is contained in an envelope and its weight, along with that of the envelope, its attachments and payload, equals or is less than that of the air it displaces, then the balloon, for that is what the device is, will fly. The gas may be a gas in its own right such as hydrogen, helium or coal gas, or ordinary air that has been heated in order to reduce its density.

Eventually the penny dropped and on 21 November 1783, following a number of unmanned and tethered experiments, a hot air balloon carrying the world's first aeronauts ascended in free flight from the Chateau La Muette, Paris. Built by the brothers Joseph and Etienne Montgolfier and flown by François Pilâtre de Rozier and the Marquis d'Arlandes, that potential fire hazard made of paper and fuelled by a mixture of wool and straw remained aloft for some twenty-five minutes, covered a distance of about two miles, and landed safely.

Early hot air balloons suffered from numerous disadvantages, limited endurance and the risk of fire being those most frequently quoted, although the prospect of encountering rain whilst flying a paper aircraft must have been somewhat daunting. It is hardly surprising, therefore, that with one exception, to be described later, they fell into disuse for about 150 years until twentieth century materials led to their resurgence.

Strange to relate, only ten days elapsed before a quite different type of balloon rose from the Tuileries Gardens into the Paris sky. It was a hydrogen-filled gas balloon crewed by its designer, Prof. J.A.C. Charles, and one of its constructors M. Aine Robert. They too landed safely. Charles almost achieved a perfect design from the outset, most modern gas balloons differing only in detail from the original. A typical gas balloon consists of an approximately spherical envelope of rubberised silk, or some similar material, with an open-ended neck at the bottom, through which gas can escape as it expands with temperature and pressure changes, and a valve at the top, through which it can be discharged at the will of the aeronaut. The envelope is contained in a net to the bottom of which is attached a horizontally mounted hoop from which the car or basket is suspended. The balloon can be made to climb by dropping ballast, usually sand, and to descend by valving gas.

Balloon ascents soon began to take place outside France. The first in Great Britain was made at Edinburgh by James Tytler using a rudimentary hot air balloon on 25 August 1784. It was but a short hop and he was fortunate to survive the experience. There followed a more successful ascent, the first in England, by Vincenzo Lunardi, an Italian, who flew a hydrogen balloon from Moorfields, London, to Ware, Hertfordshire, on 15 September. The first Englishman to fly in England, James Sadler, ascended from Oxford in a hot air balloon on 4 October. He repeated the feat, also at Oxford, using a hydrogen balloon on 12 November.

Balloons soon became part of showbusiness. In Great Britain, ascents from the pleasure gardens of London became a regular feature of nineteenth-century metropolitan life and, as rail communications spread, allowing aeronauts to travel the country with relative ease, provincial citizens were treated to similar exhibitions. Balloons were also utilised for military observation, scientific research, and occasionally for pleasure, although the 'golden age' of sport ballooning did not commence until Edwardian times.

Aeronautics took some time to arrive in Glamorgan due to the fact that, until the Industrial Revolution, the county was a sparsely populated agricultural area. The census of 1801 gave the population of Merthyr Tydfil, the largest town in the county, and in Wales, as 7,705; Swansea came second with 6,831 while Cardiff could muster a mere 1,870 people. As the century progressed, however, industrialisation advanced at a rapid pace and the character of the county was changed beyond recognition. This can be illustrated by comparing these figures with those of the 1881 census, which gave the population of Merthyr Tydfil and district as 101,441 and Swansea as 93,001, both of which had been eclipsed by Cardiff whose population had swelled to 106,164. The progress of local aeronautics was to a considerable extent allied to that expansion.

The first attempts at manned flights in the county were made at Swansea by one Francis Barrett, using a hydrogen balloon in October 1802. Barrett, a long forgotten would-be aeronaut, had achieved a measure of notoriety on 13 August of that year when, after an unsuccessful attempted ascent from Greenwich, he had been obliged to release his balloon unmanned to save it from the ravages of rioting spectators.

Determined to make a successful ascent and achieve the fame and fortune attendant thereupon, he chose Swansea as the venue for his next attempt and arrived in the town by packet from Devon on 31 August, some weeks ahead of the balloon which was transported by road. He was not idle during those weeks. In order to stimulate interest in his forthcoming exploit he gave two public demonstrations of unmanned hot air balloons from a stage in front of the George Inn. The first balloon, some 20ft high and 18ft diameter, was constructed of tissue paper and intended to bear aloft two parachutists, in the form of a cat and a small dog; the parachute from which their cage was suspended was attached to the balloon by a slow burning fuse. That ambitious example of early aeromodelling came to naught when a combination of high wind and a jammed release line resulted in the balloon being destroyed by fire on lift off. The fate of its occupants is not recorded. Some days later, however, he successfully demonstrated two smaller balloons that remained aloft for nearly ten minutes and covered a distance of about 200 yards.

When the full-sized balloon arrived it was exhibited on two occasions, inflated with air, inside the ball court of the George Inn. According to Barrett his receipts from admission charges amounted to £1 6s and his outlay on hire of the court and labour to £4 12s 2½d – hardly a profitable undertaking. Despite that inauspicious start he managed to persuade several local businessmen to subscribe the sum of £70 to finance the intended flight. The potential profit from gate money was enormous.

The widely advertised ascent was scheduled for Wednesday 6 October. It was reported that a crowd of some 8,000 people assembled at the launch site and, according to *The Times*, 'the fields, the hills, the houses, the ships in the harbour, every place was crowded with people from the most distant parts of the country – the town was never so full.' Preparations commenced at 8.00 a.m. The balloon was erected on a stage and inflation began. As was usual at that time the hydrogen was manufactured in situ by pouring sulphuric acid, or vitriol as it was more commonly known, into barrels containing iron filings, the gas given off being fed to the neck of the envelope via a number of tin pipes. The result of those labours, however, turned out to be a recurrence of the Greenwich fiasco, leakage of gas from the pipes, and possibly the balloon itself, precluded a full inflation. Barrett sent to the local chemist for more acid but, as his finances were exhausted, that worthy refused to augment his supply. By 3.00 p.m. the crowd had become unruly and Barrett mounted the stage in order to calm the situation. 'Ladies and Gentlemen', he began – and finished, for at that moment the stage collapsed precipitating the balloon, Barrett and his helpers to the ground. He was barely able to prevent the second riot of his aeronautical career, only the promise of another attempt at a later date resulted in the balloon being spared, leaving the unfortunate aeronaut to foot the bill, which by then included a fee for the setting of a small boy's leg broken in the accident.

The second attempt took place on Friday 15 October. The inflation of the envelope, which had been revarnished in the interval, again commenced at 8.00 a.m. but by 4.00 p.m., when the car was attached, it was by no means full. A few minutes later, however, some 50lb of ballast was loaded and an optimistic Barrett climbed aboard, clutching a bottle of brandy and a pound of mutton wrapped in a pocket handkerchief, 'in case of descending where no meat was to be had.' The order 'let go' was given – and nothing happened, some ballast was jettisoned – to no effect, the remaining ballast and the mutton followed at which point *Barrett's Balloon* became the first manned aircraft to ascend from Glamorgan – albeit briefly. It rose to a height of about 60ft, drifted across the field and, despite the jettisoning of the brandy, descended into a row of trees, the first of many arboreal encounters to grace these pages. No damage was done, however, and willing helpers dragged the balloon back to its starting point where it was again released. Once more it rose half-heartedly into the air as the aeronaut waved his cap to the onlookers but, being no lighter than on the previous occasion, it fared no better, only remaining airborne sufficiently to cross four fields before making a gentle touchdown. For the next fifteen minutes it hopped and skipped over fields and hedges until the exasperated Barrett leaped from the car, whereupon is shot rapidly upwards and reportedly achieved a great height before eventually returning to earth in a field about six miles distant where it was discovered by two local labourers who amicably resolved their respective claims to ownership by cutting it in half.

What was probably the first balloon to grace the skies of east Glamorgan appeared in the afternoon of Monday 24 September 1810. It was a gas balloon that had ascended from Stokes Croft, Bristol, under the command of the first English aeronaut, James Sadler. He was accompanied by William Clayfield, 'a gentleman distinguished for his chemical knowledge, and of great respectability', and a cat that subsequently departed by parachute and survived. The two aeronauts settled down to what promised to be an uneventful channel crossing to South Wales. An observer on the top of Cardiff Castle, then a ruin prior to its spectacular reconstruction by the Marquis of Bute, reported in a letter to *The Times*, that the green and purple balloon and its two occupants could be clearly discerned through a glass as it approached the coast at Cardiff. However, just as a safe landing on Welsh soil seemed assured, the wind shifted and, despite attempts by Sadler to regain track by changing height,

Sadler's descent into the Bristol Channel. (Cuthbert Collection, Royal Aeronautical Society)

the balloon was carried along the coast just off Sully, Barry, Rhoose and Aberthaw, where it took up a southerly track and began to descend. Their ballast exhausted, the aeronauts jettisoned all loose articles including their coats and a cherished barometer, a gift to Sadler from Dr Johnson valued at 200 guineas, to no avail. Finally they donned lifebelts and awaited the inevitable encounter with the sea, which took place some five miles off Lynmouth after a flight of about three hours. They spent a further hour clinging to the balloon as it was driven across the surface of the water by the wind, before being picked up by a boat and landed at Lynmouth, little the worse for the experience.

Due to the small population in the early nineteenth century, local newspaper coverage was sparse, and it is probable that a number of ascents took place at that time that have gone unrecorded. For example, the Street Commissioners Minutes for Cardiff contain an entry to the effect that on 20 November 1828 the gas company was excused from lighting the streets in order to supply gas for Mr Green's balloon. No record of such a flight exists. Mr Green was probably Charles Green, a London fruiterer, and the doyen of nineteenth-century British aeronauts who, between 1821 and 1852, made over 500 ascents. He also pioneered the use of coal gas for balloon inflation. Although heavier and of less predictable quality than pure hydrogen necessitating the use of larger balloons, coal gas was much less expensive and, with increasing urbanisation, readily available. It was only necessary to tap into a convenient gas main, preferably with the gas company's approval, to inflate a balloon. A newspaper article, containing several inaccuracies, written at the end of the century, credits Charles Green with having made a number of ascents from Cardiff, including one where he was compelled to climb up the netting onto the crown of the envelope to free the valve which had jammed. I have only discovered records of one of those ascents, Green's 369th made in his balloon *The Royal Victoria* on Monday 9 August 1847 from Mr Pritchard's field at the bottom of St Mary Street, a spot very near the present Penarth Road railway bridge.

The inflation under the supervision of Mr Bowen, the chief engineer of Cardiff Gas Works, commenced at 11.00 a.m. An estimated 1,000 people travelled to Cardiff on special trains laid on by the Taff Vale Railway Co. and some 1,200 paid 1*s* 6*d* admission to watch the balloon take shape to the accompaniment of the Cardiff Amateur Band playing fashionable pieces of the day. Others, however, elected to save their money and view the proceedings gratis from the roofs of surrounding buildings. That served only to add to the entertainment when a house, upon whose roof a crowd had assembled, collapsed with a loud crash leaving a pile of moaning bodies amid the debris.

Shortly after 6.00 p.m. Green and his brother treated the population to that most beautiful of all aerial spectacles – the silent ascent of a free gas balloon. It was a sight that so moved one local bard that he penned the following lines subsequently published in the *Cardiff and Merthyr Guardian*:

> *The beauteous Orb ascends!*
> *The veterans take their leave –*
> *Heav'nward the vision wends,*
> *While earthly bosoms heave:-*
> *And Wallia's sons and daughters fair*
> *Greet them with cheers that rend the air.*

Charles Green's balloon Royal Victoria *which ascended from Cardiff on 9 August 1847.* (Author's collection)

> *How tranquilly they leave!*
> *They move the heav'ns along!*
> *The fields of ether cleve,*
> *Their way the clouds among:-*
> *A passing thought succeeds – a sigh!*
> *A last farewell! lone speck on high.*

The flight terminated safely at Nailsea, near Bristol, the balloon having covered about thirty miles in fifty minutes.

Only four weeks later, on 6 September, another noted aeronaut, Richard Gypson, ascended from the Post Office Field, Merthyr Tydfil, in his balloon *The Royal Albert*. Such was the excitement generated by the event that all shops in the town closed at 4.00 p.m. and between 800 and 1,000 people paid admission to the field which, as far as can be ascertained, was situated immediately to the east of High Street, between John Street and the present railway station. Thousands more, of course, viewed the event gratis from the surrounding hills. As was becoming customary at that time places in the basket, at a fee, were on offer to the public.

In the event Gypson ascended alone probably due to the nationwide publicity that had attended an ascent from the Vauxhall Gardens, London, some two months previously. On that occasion, a night ascent with fireworks, the balloon had been sucked upwards into a thunderstorm and burst, precipitating Gypson and his three companions from 4,000ft into a

Pimlico building site. Only a fortuitous encounter with some scaffolding which snagged the balloon net and arrested their descent saved them from probable annihilation.

After some delay due to difficulties with the gas supply, Gypson ascended at about 7.00 p.m. After a relatively short flight, during which he experienced considerable buffeting from the heat rising from local furnaces, he landed safely at Cefn Forest.

A similar exhibition incorporating a fireworks display, held in a field adjoining the Theatre, Crockherbtown, Cardiff, the site now occupied by Eglwys Dewi Sant, St Andrews Crescent, had a more bizarre conclusion. The ascent was advertised for Monday 9 July 1849 and the promoter and owner of the balloon *Rainbow*, Mr W. Wadman of Montpelier, Bristol, stated that the aeronaut Mr R. Green, a thirty-two-year-old Birmingham man, would drop a live animal by parachute. Places in the basket were again on offer.

Again Mr Bowen supervised the inflation and the Cardiff Amateur Band provided the entertainment. The evening was fine and clear with a light northerly wind and many members of the public paid for admission to the field although none availed themselves of the opportunity to ascend. Green's sole companion, therefore, was the parachutist – a reluctant cat. 'Pussy remonstrated with all the power of her lungs and claws against being made a party to the exhibition', reported the *Cardiff and Merthyr Guardian*, but nevertheless was tied in a net attached to the parachute. A pilot balloon was released and drifted in a southerly direction indicating that a channel crossing was in prospect. Green ascended on schedule and, as anticipated, *Rainbow* took up a southerly track. The parachute was dropped and deposited the unfortunate cat, 'more frightened than hurt', upon the deck of a vessel in Bute Docks.

Having spent some time becalmed off Penarth the balloon was then borne on a light wind towards Portishead, remaining visible to the spectators for an hour and a quarter. They then turned their attention to the forthcoming fireworks display oblivious to the drama that was being enacted above the channel. The wind that evening was obviously light and very variable in direction for, before reaching Portishead, the balloon began to track back down the channel in a south-westerly direction. It passed quite close to the English and Welsh Grounds lightship, whose master hailed Green by megaphone and asked if he required assistance. The reply was unintelligible. Eventually *Rainbow* turned towards Sand Bay, near Weston-super-Mare, where local farmer Mr John Gill watched it descend on the northern side of Sand Point. He summoned two boys and together they ran to offer assistance. Before they reached the scene, however, they saw the balloon rise rapidly on the seaward side of the point, indicative of a great weight loss. It initially moved towards Clevedon then turned inland and was lost to view. It was discovered the following morning undamaged and still inflated near Wedmore, Somerset. The basket still contained many heavy items including a grapnel, ropes, ballast bags and Green's coat and boots weighing in all about 85lb. Of Green there was no sign.

It can only be assumed that as the balloon was wafted off the shore by the light and variable winds he had despaired of ever reaching land before dusk and had committed one of the cardinal sins of aeronautics – he panicked. It is probable that when he got near the coast he valved *Rainbow* down to sea level, jumped from the basket and tried to swim ashore, a feat that John Gill reckoned to be impossible due to local currents. Had he stayed with the balloon, as events proved, he could have climbed to a higher altitude and found an onshore breeze.

It was the same John Gill who discovered the decomposed body of a man at Sand Bay at 6.00 p.m. on Wednesday 25 July, some sixteen days after the incident. Acting in accordance with the standing orders of the District Coroner, he summoned some local farmers to view it, obtained a coffin, and with no attempt at identification, the remains, which were almost certainly those of Green, were interred in the churchyard of St Pauls, Kewstoke, at 10.00 p.m. the same evening in a nocturnal ceremony conducted by the vicar of Kewstoke, Revd R.C. Hathway. An inquest held some days later merely returned a verdict of 'Found drowned'.

Green's tragic end seemed to dampen public enthusiasm for balloons for there appear to have been few ascents in the district until 26 September 1860 when Henry Coxwell, a veteran aeronaut who had been one of Gypson's companions in the Pimlico fiasco, ascended from a fête at Canton Market, Cardiff. The site at the end of Market Street is, at the time of writing, occupied by The Chapter Arts Centre.

The ascent was one of the last by Coxwell's famous balloon *Mars*, then nearing the end of its useful life. Due to the northerly wind, Coxwell elected to terminate the flight after only half an hour, landing in the vicinity of Westra, Dinas Powys.

As previously stated, the heyday of sporting ballooning did not occur until Edwardian times. Nevertheless, there were a few individuals who flew solely for pleasure prior to then – among them Walter Powell MP, the son of Thomas Powell the founder of the Powell Duffryn industrial empire. On 22 November 1881 Powell, who was a guest of Mr Charles Williams of Llanrumney Hall, ascended in his 28,500cu.ft balloon *Day Star* from Grangetown Gas Works, Cardiff. After an uneventful flight he and his unnamed companion landed near Cirencester an hour and three quarters later.

This was one of his last flights for, on 10 December 1881, he was carried out to sea and lost without trace in the military balloon *Saladin* after its commander, Capt. James Templer RE and another occupant had been thrown from the basket following an extremely heavy landing near Bridport, Dorset.

Another aeronaut whose days were numbered was Joseph Simmons, a fifty-four-year-old civil engineer and veteran of some 500 ascents, who piloted the balloon *Rookwood* from Manselton Racecourse, Swansea, on 21 May 1888. The balloon was the main attraction at a fête held in celebration of the silver wedding anniversary of the Prince and Princess of Wales and was billed as 'The Great War Balloon', possibly due to the fact that it was inflated from cylinders of compressed hydrogen, a method that had been employed by the army since 1884.

Simmons amazed the crowd by climbing above the southerly sea breeze and finding the northerly gradient wind, which carried him to a safe landing at Simonsbath, near Porlock.

Sadly his thirty-year aeronautical career ended only three months later when he was killed in a landing accident at Utting, Essex, following an ascent from The Irish Exhibition at Olympia.

2

Changing Times

The latter years of the nineteenth century saw several advances in the aeronautical field, one of the more significant being the development of the flexible parachute. Parachutes had been used for many years prior to that; the first descent from a balloon over Paris was made on 22 October 1797 by the French aeronaut A.J. Garnerin, who also made the first descent in Great Britain over London on 21 September 1802. However, the parachutes used by Garnerin and his imitators were rigid structures, whose design owed a great deal to that of the umbrella. They were unstable, uncontrollable and prone to structural failure and several very public fatal accidents led to their use being frowned upon by the authorities.

The concept of a parachute relying solely on air pressure to maintain its shape evolved in the United States c.1887. The first practical example was produced by P.A. Van Tassel, an American domiciled Dutchman, who wisely delegated its testing to former circus acrobat and tightrope walker, Thomas Scott Baldwin. Baldwin made several descents before falling out with Van Tassel and teaming up with G.A. Farini to produce a much improved design. The Baldwin-Farini parachute, a design that inspired many imitators and remained in use for about twenty-five years, introduced the familiar silken mushroom shaped canopy that is still in use today but differed from modern parachutes in most other respects. The parachute was not stored in any sort of pack, merely hung from the balloon, neither was it attached to the parachutist by a harness. He or she merely gripped a trapeze bar attached to the rigging lines and sat in a webbing sling that hung from the bar. Many parachutists took the added precaution of attaching themselves to the trapeze bar by means of a lanyard and quick release clips. Although not as steerable as modern parachutes, limited directional control could be exercised by hauling on the rigging lines and spilling air from the canopy, although the surest way of landing on a suitable spot was to drop at the right time and place.

Baldwin arrived in Britain in the summer of 1888 and announced his intention of giving an exhibition in the grounds of the Alexandra Palace, London. Despite considerable misgivings being expressed in Parliament and elsewhere he ascended from the Palace grounds in the evening of 28 July and landed safely. In the course of the following few months he went on to make about a dozen descents in London, Manchester and Birmingham, earned national acclaim, the Gold Medal of the Balloon Club and, the ultimate seal of approval, an exhibition by Royal Command before the Prince and Princess of Wales. Unlike many others, Baldwin did well out of aeronautics and remained a wealthy man until his death from natural causes in 1923.

Where Baldwin led others followed and balloon ascents and parachute descents became popular attractions at outdoor events until the outbreak of the First World War. The early practitioners of that little chronicled and practically forgotten activity, like Baldwin, came mostly from circus backgrounds. Many were female, there was added attraction in watching a pretty young girl risk her neck, and the circus tradition of flamboyant costumes and exotic pseudonyms and titles was the norm.

Various methods of elevating parachutists were employed. The most common was a small gas balloon of about 20,000cu.ft that could be filled from any convenient gas main. The apex of the parachute was attached to the balloon netting near the envelope's equator by a piece of weak string, the parachutist's weight being taken by a seat below the balloon. It was only necessary to slide from the seat to break the string and fall free. A drop of about a 100ft was sufficient to open the canopy but, due to the rapid ascent of the lightened balloon, it appeared much greater when viewed from the ground. A weight attached to the top of the balloon caused it to invert, vent its gas, and fall to earth for recovery and reuse.

Where gas was unavailable simple hot air balloons, sometimes known as smoke balloons, were used. Those most exciting of all balloons consisted of little more than muslin bags which, unlike either early Montgolfiers or modern hot air balloons, carried no self-contained source of heat. Their inflation kept many people occupied for the best part of a day and, even more than that of gas balloons, was an entertainment in itself. The envelope was hung from a rope between two poles with its mouth above the end of a long trench filled with combustible materials and covered as far as the balloon mouth with corrugated iron sheets. The contents of the trench were ignited and, as the hot air entered the balloon and it became self-supporting, the poles and rope were removed and the parachute attached. When the parachutist judged the balloon to be sufficiently buoyant, its mouth was pulled shut by means of a draw-string and it was liberated by an axe-wielding assistant. The initial rate of ascent was startling – a height of 3,000ft being achieved in two minutes or less – but the balloon would cool rapidly and lose lift leaving the parachutist a limited time in which to drop. As the balloon inverted it released a cloud of black smoke, hence the name smoke balloon.

Parachutists, sometimes several at a time, also ascended perched on the rims of the baskets of larger balloons which became known as right away balloons – because they flew right away from the showground. In such cases, if weight permitted, the aeronaut could supplement his income by carrying fare-paying passengers in the basket. Around the turn of the century a simple quick-release mechanism incorporating a cotter pin was devised. It allowed the parachute to be attached directly to the bottom of the envelope of a solo balloon or to the underside of the basket of right away balloons – the parachutist's weight needing no other support than that provided by the sling. Separation of parachute and balloon was achieved by pulling out the pin by means of a hand line. Despite several exciting malfunctions, miraculously none fatal, the system was widely adopted.

The Annual Foresters Fête Gala and Sports held at Ynysangharad Fields, Pontypridd, on Whit Monday 26 May 1890, afforded South Walians the opportunity to witness the first of many memorable, not to say hair-raising, parachute descents that took place in the course of the following two decades. The parachutist, Miss Ida MacDonald, was a member of a well-known show business family who had, according to publicity statements, been involved in aeronautics for some time. For reasons that are obscure she used a hot air balloon, a device with which neither she nor her assistants had had any previous experience. Nevertheless the inflation proceeded smoothly and shortly after 7.00 p.m. the balloon was tugging at its restraints with the parachute attached, its canopy and cords laid horizontally across the grass. Miss MacDonald, clad in a white lambswool suit, attached herself to the parachute and sat upon a small wicker seat that was hoisted clear of the ground by two helpers. One can only assume that they were anticipating a slow ascent, characteristic of a gas balloon, that would have allowed them to walk the parachutist to a point below the envelope as it climbed away. They were shortly to be disabused of any such notion.

On receipt of the command 'Let go' the balloon was liberated and the ensuing chain of events can only be surmised by interpreting the garbled accounts of two horrified journalists who witnessed the spectacle. It would appear that the balloon's departure was somewhat reminiscent of that of a champagne cork. All concerned were taken by surprise, the seat was snatched from the hands of the helpers and its occupant pitched out and borne rapidly aloft either clinging to or tangled in the balloon rigging, probably the seat attachment cords. Worse was to come when the parachute canopy became detached from the balloon envelope and dangled limply below the parachutist who, as the balloon cooled, was left with little option other than to drop and trust to luck – a commodity that was in short supply that evening. She fell onto the canopy and apparently spent some time tangled in it as she plummeted earthwards. Eventually she freed herself from the flapping silk allowing the parachute to open – albeit imperfectly. The spectators in the fields and the thousands more who had assembled on the common could only watch in horror as the white figure, gyrating wildly under the influence of the untwisting cords, thudded into a field between Ynysangharad House and the River Taff. Many thousands of would-be rescuers rushed to the scene fearing the worst but were amazed to find the girl lying on her back in the grass thanking God for her deliverance. That task complete, she fainted. Remarkably, with the exception of a dislocated ankle, some bruising and 'a severe shock to the system', she was little the worse for the adventure. The balloon was later recovered from a hedge at Gelliwion Farm but it is doubtful if Miss MacDonald ever used it again, for although she topped the bill at the following year's Foresters Fête at Pontypridd it was in her previous capacity of high wire artiste.

Another former circus performer turned aeronaut who spent some time in the county during the inclement summer of 1891 was 'Professor' Alec MacKay, billed as 'The Original and Only Gymnast Parachutist', whose aerial antics are best described as bordering on the incredible. Having dropped from his 16,000cu.ft gas balloon *Queen of the Isles*, it was his wont to occupy the time spent in descent performing gymnastic feats on the trapeze.

His first performance, at a sports meeting at the Central Athletic Grounds, William Street, Swansea, was adjudged to have been an unqualified success. A land breeze necessitated a fairly short flight in order to ensure a touchdown on dry land but even so, having thrilled the crowd with his act, he only just managed to keep his feet dry, landing on railway sidings near the South Dock. *Queen of the Isles* fell into the sea near the Pier Head and was retrieved, along with a small boy who had got into difficulties while attempting to swim to her, by the crew of a small boat.

There was considerable parachuting activity in South Wales over the period of the August Bank Holiday, with successful performances by Miss Merton at Llanelli on Saturday 1 August and by Herr Grais at Newport, Monmouthshire, on Monday 3 August. 'Professor' MacKay, however, was thwarted in an attempt to ascend from the Oddfellow Annual Fete and Gala at the Sophia Gardens, Cardiff, on the blustery, showery Monday afternoon. The balloon was inflated to the accompaniment of the odd peal of thunder but developed a tear and the ascent had to be abandoned. It developed several more tears when it was set upon by an angry mob of disappointed spectators, a common occurrence in those days.

A performance at the same venue at a fête in aid of the Great Western Railway Widows and Orphans Fund on Saturday 15 August was attended by better fortune. On that occasion, MacKay concluded his descent hanging by his toes from the trapeze; in that extraordinary position he crashed through the branches of a tree in nearby Cathays Park, yet somehow contrived to arrive uninjured on terra firma. *Queen of the Isles* was once again recovered from the sea by a pilot cutter off Clevedon.

'Professor' MacKay's busy schedule then took him back to Swansea for a week of performances in connection with the Welsh National Eisteddfod but the rain and high winds that caused part of the eisteddfod pavilion to collapse, killing a woman member of the audience, precluded any further ascents. Alec MacKay then seems to have left the area and faded into obscurity.

As the century drew to a close, a change crept over the face of aeronautics worldwide. The circus image was superseded by one of staid responsibility. Professional balloon pilots adopted the title of 'captain' and circus costumes were replaced by uniforms. In fact, the dress and traditions of the present Merchant Air Service have their roots in that period. Male uniform, then as now, closely resembled that of Merchant Navy officers with the addition of balloon motifs on lapels and caps. Females wore navy blue knickerbocker suits with sailor collars, calf length boots and high peaked caps. Although a practical form of dress for strenuous outdoor activities, knickerbockers were considered by many to be at best daring and at worst indecent attire for women. However, although numerous pioneer lady cyclists and others were arraigned before magistrates for wearing them, it appears that no parachutist suffered the same fate, probably because nobody could think of a more decent alternative.

In the United Kingdom aeronautics came increasingly under the influence of one family, the Spencers, a remarkable dynasty whose activities spanned four generations and nearly a century. The founding father, Edward Spencer, a solicitor and lifelong friend of Charles Green, had named his son Charles Green Spencer after the great man. He, in turn, founded the firm of C.G. Spencer & Sons of Highbury, London, manufacturers and operators of balloons and, as time went by, parachutes and airships too. The third generation of Spencer brothers, the generation that feature in this tale, together with their brother-in-law, the London-domiciled Frenchman Auguste Gaudron had, by the turn of the century, acquired a near monopoly of British civil aeronautics. As the firm of C.G. Spencer expanded it employed balloonists and parachutists from outside the family, some of the latter being 'adopted daughters' – young women who assumed the Spencer surname as a pseudonym possibly to conceal their activities from parents and loved ones.

Another innovation was the adoption of the military observation balloon as a civilian joy riding craft. Tethered to a steam winch, it could be filled with fare-paying passengers, allowed to rise to 1,000ft or so and be hauled back to earth again, providing the passengers with a far greater thrill than any fairground ride. One such balloon, the 56,000cu.ft *Excellent*, under the command of Capt. Stanley Spencer, was the principal attraction at the Cardiff Horticultural Society's sixth annual show held at the Sophia Gardens on 15 and 16 August 1894. As a local journalist later wrote, 'If only the public could have been advised in advance of the outcome of its one and only ascent the show's attendance figures would have been greatly enhanced.'

The first day's flying was abandoned due to inclement weather and it was not until Thursday 16 August that the balloon was inflated. Even so, Spencer was reluctant to ascend

The rise and fall of the balloon
Excellent *at Sophia Gardens,*
Cardiff, 16 August 1894.

1. Climbing down the tree out of the car.   2. Filling the balloon in the Park.
3. The balloon ascending after bursting.

due to the strong, gusty wind that swept across the gardens. Finally, however, he made an error that all fliers should guard against, he yielded to pressure from others who wanted to see some action. The show committee prevailed on Spencer to make a trial ascent carrying themselves as passengers and he reluctantly agreed. At a little after 4.00 p.m. *Excellent*, its basket containing Spencer and that foolhardy band Messrs W.C. Peace (Chairman), H.B. Crouch (Vice Chairman), H. Gillett (Secretary), T. Beames, F.G. Treseder, A.J. Beer, E.A. Williams and W. Lucas, ascended from the gardens and rose to the end of its tether. Having viewed their home territory from above, probably for the first time in their lives, the time came for the party to descend and the winchman commenced to draw in the cable. I feel that it would be futile to attempt to describe their return to earth in any other words than those of the gleeful *Western Mail* reporter who witnessed it:

> *Soon, however, the efforts of the engine proved superfluous, for suddenly, with no reason apparent for those on land, the balloon began to descend rapidly. By this time the exuberance of the party aboard had overtaken Bob Acres's courage, the waving of handkerchiefs ceased and as they*

came in sight of terra firma their countenances appeared 'sicklied o'er with the pale cast of thought.' The balloon swooped down and ripped itself on a large tree, breaking off some of the branches, the car striking the ground – a thrilling moment which one of the party utilised to make a leap for life, fortunately getting off without injury. The others, less prompt or more cautious, hung on and were carried upwards again about 60 yards (according to the estimate of one onlooker). Then the wayward car with its demoralised balloon wandered over the lake and in the park beyond the gardens embraced another tree – this preposterous car seems to have a striking penchant for trees – and lodged there. The sight was grotesque, for the half dozen committee men crouched in the car appeared like birds of a strange and peculiar shape, huddled in an extraordinary nest, and the crowd below gave vent to the suppressed excitement of the previous 'mauvre quatre heure' in long loud and unbridled mirth. The descent was not easily made. The chairman made the running in clambering out of the car onto the tree, and hanging there appealed in piteous terms to a 'limb of the law' to fetch him off the limb of the tree. Some of his colleagues climbed down hand over fist recalling Darwin's 'Origin of Species'. Others had to be helped down, so limp and washed out were they while secretary Gillett reminded one of the fate which so often overtakes those 'who in quarrels interpose'.

Needless to say that was the end of flying for the day, the damage to *Excellent* being estimated at £300.

3

The Flight of Mademoiselle Albertina

A considerably larger affair than the Cardiff Horticultural Show, the Cardiff Fine Arts Industrial and Maritime Exhibition was held in neighbouring Cathays Park during the summer of 1896, some years before the construction of the present Civic Centre commenced. Opened on 2 May by its president the Rt Hon. Lord Windsor, it ran for six months and attracted nearly 900,000 visitors including the Prince of Wales, who received the freedom of the borough at a ceremony in the main exhibition hall. The exhibition occupied the entire park, the exhibits being housed in a number of imposing pavilions at the south side, the rest of the site being given over to a variety of other attractions including a funfair, a boating lake which doubled as the setting for 'Santiago', a spectacular open air opera, and water pageant and a sports arena incorporating what was claimed to be the finest bicycle racetrack in the world.

Throughout the summer, the organisers laid on a varied programme of evening entertainments and it was almost inevitable that there would be some aeronautical content. When they engaged the services of 'Professor' A.E. Gaudron to make a series of balloon ascents and parachute descents during the week commencing 13 July they unwittingly ensured that the Cardiff Exhibition would be remembered for a long time, but not for the reasons they would have preferred.

Although only twenty-seven years old, Auguste Eugene Gaudron had acquired a wealth of aeronautical experience since commencing an apprenticeship as a balloon maker in his native France at the age of twelve. After marrying into the famous Spencer family and settling in London, he had become well known throughout the country as a balloonist and parachutist.

It was a week of mixed fortunes for Gaudron. On Monday 13 July, suspended below a 15,000cu.ft gas balloon, he rose from the sports arena, a site now occupied by the main building of the University College and subsequently floated down to a somewhat uncomfortable landing on an outhouse roof at the rear of Janet Street, Splott. The balloon sustained damage in an encounter with a glass-topped wall and could not be repaired in time for the next advertised ascent on Wednesday. A spare envelope was produced but developed a leak and failed to inflate sufficiently to lift the aeronaut who decided to abandon the ascent. He dropped from his seat and inadvertently initiated a farcial spectacle when the buoyancy of the partly filled envelope took his helpers by surprise. The capricious balloon tore itself from their grasp and set off across the exhibition grounds towards the town centre, where it caused a considerable commotion when it landed outside the north entrance of the Queen Street Arcade. What was to have been the final performance took place on Friday 17 July when the 'Professor' was deposited in the East Dock and the balloon in the Penarth Road timber float. Having been fished from the dock by some of his compatriots, the crew of the sailing ship *Long Cours*, of Nantes, and fortified with a quantity of Bordeaux, he returned to the exhibition ground in a cab, the door of which was smashed as the crowd clamoured to give him a hero's welcome.

Such was the appeal of Gaudron's displays that the organisers retained his services for a further week. The Monday newspapers carried advertisements to that effect, adding that on Tuesday, Thursday and Friday ascents would be made by the celebrated lady parachutist Mademoiselle Albertina, thus ensuring a performance every evening. Monday evening's ascent went well followed by an uneventful landing in a field at the end of Albany Road, the balloon terminating its flight at Llanedeyrn. Continued success seemed assured on Tuesday when a wet afternoon gave way to a fine evening with a stiff westerly breeze and a large crowd passed through the turnstiles to witness the Cardiff debut of Mademoiselle Albertina.

At a quarter to eight she made her entrance. A contemporary report described her as looking young and diminutive with refined features and girlish blue eyes. She wore the standard lady parachutist's uniform over which was secured a cork lifejacket. She took her seat amid loud applause and, preparations complete, the balloon was liberated. As it rose she called to a young man who she obviously knew 'Don't forget the milk' and then, with a wave to the crowd and a cheerful shout of 'Goodbye tra la la', she was borne rapidly out of their midst.

Thousands of people watched the progress of the balloon as it tracked across Roath, climbing rapidly until by the time it was above Tremorfa it had attained an estimated height of 6,000ft, far higher than Gaudron had ever risen. It was at that point that the parachutist, by then only discernible as a tiny speck, dropped. The canopy blossomed above her to the accompaniment of enthusiastic cheers from the crowd at the exhibition ground. Elation soon turned to concern, however, when it became apparent that Mademoiselle Albertina had made a serious error of judgment in allowing herself to be carried so high and so far to the east. People at East Moors watched helplessly as she drifted over their heads and over the mudflats to alight in the Bristol Channel off the mouth of the Rhymney River. The deflated balloon dropped onto the mudflats and was recovered by a large crowd of people.

For the rest of the evening confusion reigned supreme as attempts were made to ascertain the girl's fate. Gaudron took a cab to the Moors and questioned a number of eyewitnesses including two men who had been fishing from boats and who had witnessed the descent. One stated that while rowing towards the estimated point of touchdown he saw a three-masted schooner heave to in the area before putting about and setting course for Clevedon. His story was corroborated by the second man who had rowed into the area after the schooner had departed. He had found no trace of the girl and had concluded that she had been picked up by the vessel and would either be landed at Clevedon or transferred to a ship bound for Newport.

A relieved Gaudron returned to the exhibition ground at a quarter to ten and having passed on his findings to the anxious crowd, settled down to await news of the girl's landing. As the hours passed, however, and news was received of the berthing of vessels at Clevedon, Bristol and Newport, the dreadful truth dawned. Mademoiselle Albertina had not been picked up by any ship and was still out in the dark waters of the Channel.

As morning dawned all hope that Mademoiselle Albertina might be alive had faded and attempts were made to recover her body. The tug *Cormorant* proceeded to the estimated point of touchdown and commenced grappling among the stakes of fishing nets that covered the area to no avail. Meanwhile worried exhibition organisers forbade further parachuting and a shocked press and public began to ask questions about Mademoiselle Albertina's background.

The answers did not come quickly and when they did served only to send waves of shock and horror across the entire kingdom.

The first surprise came when Gaudron admitted under questioning that far from being the celebrated parachutist of the newspaper advertisements, the girl was a total novice making her first descent. He was quite frank and told all he knew about her – which did not amount to much. He explained that they had met some months previously when he and the diminutive Miss Alma Beaumont had been touring the West Country giving displays in conjunction with Messrs W.C. & S. Handock's Circus. She had been a circus employee who had taken an interest in parachuting and had looked after his equipment when it had been left at the circus ground. Her real name, he stated, was Grace Parry and he had gathered from conversations with her that she was twenty-one years old, had made a number of ascents in captive balloons, and was a cousin of Jenny Dean, a well-known parachutist. Of the rest of her family she had said little except to mention that although her mother was probably still alive she had long been out of touch with her, having been brought up by her grandmother in Bilston.

He also explained that when his contract with the circus expired, following a display at Torquay, Miss Beaumont had left his employ having decided to forsake parachuting in favour of the equally unpredictable adventure of marriage. He had advertised in West Country newspapers for a pupil parachutist to replace her but despite the lucrative fee of £5 per descent he had received no replies. However, shortly after he and his wife had arrived in Cardiff, the girl had presented herself to them having travelling from Torquay at her own expense and had offered her services. In view of her background he had employed her and, after a week's training he had judged her ready to make her first descent.

While press speculation continued, the Gaudrons made efforts to trace the girl's family. A visit to her lodgings in Edward Street yielded a single clue in the form of a letter found in the pocket of one of her dresses which bore the address 'Crinks' Tea Gardens', on the outskirts of Bristol. A journey to Bristol and a meeting with Mr and Mrs William Crinks, the proprietors of the tea gardens and, it transpired, the girl's foster parents, answered questions that had been asked on both sides of the Bristol Channel and produced a story that became a national sensation.

The Gaudrons, for their part, learned that they had been the victims of a grand deception, hardly a word of the girl's story being true. Her real name, they discovered, was Louisa Maud Evans; she had never been on a trapeze or in a balloon in her life, had been reported to the police as a missing person and, worst of all – she was only fourteen years old! The name of Grace Parry was that of Mr and Mrs Crinks' niece and Jenny Dean was neither related to nor known to the family.

The obviously distressed Crinks revealed details of Louisa's short life. Born on 6 December 1881, the daughter of a naval rating and an actress in a travelling theatre, she had been handed into their care when her mother had been forced to resume her stage career following her parents' separation. She had become so much a part of the family that she was generally known as Louie Crinks. On leaving school she had worked in a Bristol cloth factory until the spring of 1896 when Mrs Handcock, the circus proprietor, and a friend both of the Crinks' and her mother, had employed her, not as a performer as Gaudron had assumed, but as a domestic help. She had spent the summer touring with the circus until July when she left without giving notice, whereupon a worried Mrs Handock, having ascertained that she had not returned to Bristol, had reported her disappearance to the police.

The tangled web of deception explained a story that had appeared in the press attributed to a young performer in the 'Santiago' pageant by the name of J. Owen – the person to whom Louisa had called 'Don't forget the milk' as she lifted off. He had noted on the day prior to the ascent that she was visibly trembling, had enquired if anything was amiss and questioned the wisdom of ascending in such a state. She had replied 'I've got something on my mind and I'm going up. I don't care whether I come down alive or not.' The 'something' turned out to be a journalist who had been pestering her for biographical details that she was understandably reluctant to provide. She had cheered up on the day of the ascent, however, and had been humming and singing all day. Young Owen, obviously somewhat taken with her, had offered to hire a cab and pick her up after the descent. She had agreed and asked him to bring some milk saying that she always drank milk after her descents.

Louisa Evans' whereabouts remained a mystery until the evening of Friday 24 July, when fourteen-year-old Mary Waggett, who was strolling along the riverbank at Nash near Goldcliff, Newport, spied what she though to be the body of a sailor lying at the water's edge. She raised the alarm and the local constable, PC Boucher, accompanied by a group of farm workers, went to the spot and recovered what on closer inspection proved to be the body of the unfortunate parachutist. They conveyed it on a hurdle to the belfry of Nash Church where it was laid on a bier in readiness for the coroner's inquest held on the following Monday morning before Mr M. Roberts-Jones, the District Coroner.

There was some delay to the start of the proceedings held at the Waterloo Inn, Nash, in order that Mr and Mrs Crinks and Louisa's mother, with whom she had never lost touch, could complete their walk from Llanwern railway station after alighting from the Bristol train. After Mary Waggett and PC Boucher had given evidence it was the turn of the hapless Gaudron. From accounts of the proceedings it would appear that, although the coroner displayed great sympathy towards him, the jury most certainly did not. He explained the circumstances of his meeting and employing the girl and told how he had estimated the wind velocity and, with the aid of a plan of Cardiff, had briefed her to drop when above the Infirmary, thereby ensuring a safe landing near East Moors. He felt that she had delayed her descent much longer than she should have, possibly due to a fear of falling among the chimneys of the Dowlais Steel Works. He stated that he always insisted that his lady parachutists attached themselves to the parachute by means of quick release clips and, as it had not been recovered, and only one person, the deceased, could have operated the clips, the system had obviously worked successfully, despite PC Boucher's reservations as to the ability of anyone wearing a Board of Trade lifejacket to move their arms.

Mr Crinks said in evidence that 'Louisa was a girl who grew big but had an infantile face' and it was accepted that Gaudron could easily have been deceived as to her age. Medical evidence by Dr James Hurley of Newport gave the cause of death as drowning, but he opined that the lack of mud and water in her stomach indicated that she was unconscious before she entered the water. He then went on to say that as reference had been made in some quarters to the girl's virtue he ought to say that 'she was as pure a girl as ever lived and ought that might have been imputed to her was absolutely false' – a statement that brought murmured applause from his audience.

The jury, consisting of Revd R. White, Vicar of Nash, and a body of local farmers, returned a verdict that 'the deceased was accidentally drowned in the Bristol Channel on Tuesday last whilst descending from a balloon.' They were also unanimous that 'M. Gaudron displayed great carelessness and want of judgment in allowing such a young and inexperienced person to make a descent during such weather as prevailed on Tuesday last and that they wished to censure him and caution him against allowing such a thing to occur again.' At that point Gaudron broke down, turned his head to the wall and sobbed.

The jury's rider undoubtedly had an influence on local legend which has always tended to portray Gaudron as an evil monster who sent an innocent young girl to her death. It is even said that he sent her aloft that evening because he was afraid to fly himself. In my view nothing could be further from the truth. He was acknowledged by all who knew him to be a courageous and charming individual who expected no more of his employees than he did of himself. In condemning him for sending her aloft in a breeze they showed an understandable ignorance of aeronautics for, as was demonstrated by the hapless Green nearly half a century before, flight in light winds with the attendant possibility of being becalmed over inhospitable areas is far more perilous than flight in a breeze when the aeronaut is presented with a constantly varying choice of landing sites. Had she released when instructed she should have come to no harm. Dr Hurley's pronouncement that Louisa was unconscious on entering the water was typical of medical opinion of the time, which believed that a prolonged drop would render a person unconscious or even dead. In fact a prolonged drop is quite harmless – it is the sudden stop at the bottom that kills. As Gaudron pointed out, she must have been conscious to have freed herself from the parachute. The fact is that Louisa Evans entered aeronautics of her own free will and her tragic demise was due to her own error of judgment coupled by the fact that too much credence was given to the reports that she had been picked up by the ship. She was wearing a lifejacket and should not have been in any immediate danger had she not been abandoned to her fate in the face of falling darkness.

Louisa Maud Evans was buried on Wednesday 29 July amid scenes of unprecedented emotion, the expenses being met by the exhibition organisers. A crowd numbering several hundred assembled outside the Newport funeral home where her body had lain since the inquest and many more lined the route of her last journey back to Cardiff. Among the wreaths on the coffin lay the bouquet that was to have been presented to its occupant upon her triumphal return to the arena and one from Auguste Gaudron who had wisely left the district to fulfill an engagement in Glasgow. The procession proceeded to Cardiff in the face of falling drizzle, pausing briefly on St Mellons Hill in order to allow an old lady to present a wreath on behalf of local residents. Led by two mounted policemen, the cortege entered Cardiff and routed via Newport Road and Castle Road, as City Road was then known, whose residents had expressly asked that it be included in the route in order that they might pay their respects. As the vehicles passed, the crowds lining the route fell in behind them until by the time Crwys Road was reached they were followed by a vast throng. At that point one of the exhibition's main attractions, The Old World Band, joined in the proceedings playing dead marches by Mendelssohn, Schubert and Beethoven. The vast assembly, the majority of whom had not heard of Louisa Evans only a week before, finally arrived at Cathays Cemetery where a graveside service in torrential rain, conducted by Revd R.S. Plant, brought to an end what many at the time considered to be one of the most sensational episodes in Cardiff's history.

A memorial stone purchased by public subscription stands above the young aeronaut's last resting place. On it are inscribed a brief account of her demise and a tribute in verse penned by the local Inspector of Schools, Mr C.T. Whitmell:

Brave woman, yet in years a child,
Dark death closed here thy heavenward flight,
God grant thee, pure and undefiled,
To reach at last the light of light.

The grave of Louisa Maud Evans at Cathays Cemetery,
Cardiff. (Author's collection)

4
The Leonid Voyage

The final aeronautical event of the century was another Stanley Spencer spectacular, an adventure that must have tested his nerves and those of his two companions, Revd J.M. Bacon and his daughter Gertrude, to their limits.

John McKenzie Bacon, MA, FRAS, was, in the words of his daughter Gertrude, 'A most unconventional cleric'. A mathematics scholar and ordained minister of the Church of England, he had for many years combined the life of an academic with that of a clerk in holy orders until his wife's failing health led him to forsake the academic world of Cambridge and return to his native Berkshire. Having installed his family in a large house in the village of Coldash, near Newbury, he immersed himself in an extraordinary diversity of pursuits, particularly so after his wife's untimely demise.

Time not spent on pastoral duties in the nearby parish of Shaw, educating his children at home, organising flower shows, fireworks displays and youth activities, was devoted to a plethora of interests of a mainly scientific nature among them being photography, apiary, astronomy, motoring and his particular fascination, acoustics.

John Bacon's ministry spanned a particularly turbulent period in church history – a time when a head-on confrontation between science and theology seemed inevitable. Many eminent theologians of the day, doubtless fearful that their considerable authority might be undermined, regarded scientific enlightenment as an assault on the very foundations of religious faith and missed no opportunity to denounce scientific theories, on such topics as the origin of the universe or evolution, as heresy. Bacon, who found no difficulty in reconciling scientific knowledge with Christian belief, grew weary of puerile discourses as to the geographical location of Hell or the precise date and time of the creation, believing that such outmoded dogma could only lead to the loss of the Church's credibility or a return to the Dark Ages. He finally gave vent to his feelings in a pamphlet entitled *The Curse of Conventionalism: A remonstrance by a priest of the Church of England*, which so shocked the ecclesiastical establishment that he found himself ostracised by clergy and laity alike. Unrepentant, he withdrew from pastoral duties, although he remained a committed Christian for the rest of his life.

The rest of his life was devoted to exploring God's wonderful world, exploration in which the balloon played a major part. An ascent for pleasure in his younger days had convinced him that the balloon was a tool well suited to scientific observation and the first of his numerous scientific ascents was made from the grounds of Shaw House on 27 July 1898, its purpose being the study of acoustics.

The ascent that is the subject of this story was commissioned by *The Times* for the purpose of observing a shower of Leonid meteors expected to enter the atmosphere in mid-November 1899 from above cloud. In view of the fact that the balloon might have to remain inflated for several days awaiting suitable weather, Spencer, the aeronaut in charge, recommended utilising an envelope without a valve in order to minimise leakage of gas, reasoning that once aloft in the stable night air the inevitable leakage that does occur would return the balloon to earth in a few hours.

Inflation of the 56,000cu.ft balloon took place on Tuesday 14 November at Newbury Gas Works, where it remained tethered until the early hours of Thursday when Spencer deemed the weather conditions suitable for an ascent. Spencer, John Bacon and the talented and equally unconventional Gertrude embarked and the balloon ascended at 4.30 a.m., but not before a considerable quantity of ballast had been discharged to compensate for the weight of moisture that had accumulated on the envelope. Four more bags were discharged to compensate for the cooling effect of the layer of cloud through which the balloon passed and a further two to maintain the balloon in equilibrium just above the cloud tops at 3,000ft. Scientifically the flight was a disappointment, only a few meteors being seen, aeronautically it was a near disaster. As the balloon neared the cloud tops Bacon implored Spencer to empty the final sandbag in order to remain in clear air a little longer and Spencer complied – a very serious error of judgment. For the next hour to the surprise of the aeronauts the balloon lost no more height and it became apparent that Spencer's plan to land at first light had gone horribly awry.

'Battered an' shiken' – the Revd J.M. Bacon and his daughter Gertrude on 16 November 1899 after their arrival at Caerhysddu, Neath. (Author's collection)

As the sun rose, its rays illuminated a sheet of cloud that stretched as far as the eye could see, they also dried the envelope and warmed the gas contained therein causing the balloon to commence an ascent that, without the facility to valve gas, could not be controlled. Gradually the sounds of earthly activity faded – it is surprising what can be heard from a balloon even a mile or more above the ground – as the balloon continued upwards to a height of over 9,000ft. The party spent the morning and early part of the afternoon high above the cloud sheet with no idea of their position and only the vaguest idea of their direction of travel, which they correctly assumed to be westerly.

In reminiscences written at a later date, Bacon stated that they enjoyed a picnic lunch and such was the hilarity that his hat was knocked overboard – for hilarity I feel one should read hysteria. There was, in fact, considerable concern that they might suffer the same fate as Walter Powell and others who had been carried out to sea never to be seen again. At one point Spencer even considered opening the rip panel which would have collapsed the envelope and caused the balloon to plummet to earth, his reasoning being that their chances of surviving the impact were greater than their chances of surviving a ditching. Happily, he disabused himself of the notion. As the afternoon wore on the balloon began to lose height and its occupants were cheered by hearing the sound of a train and some industrial activity, which they assumed to be emanating from the Bristol area but with the benefit of hindsight probably came from Cardiff. It was at that point that Gertrude Bacon had an idea. Among the items carried in the basket was a bundle of press telegraph forms; she unwrapped it and wrote on each form the following message: 'Urgent! Large balloon from Newbury travelling overhead above the clouds. Cannot descend. Telegraph to sea coast (Coast Guards) to be ready to rescue – Bacon and Spencer.' She passed the forms to her father who folded them into three-cornered notes and, in turn, passed them to Spencer who wrote 'Urgent' on them in red chalk and dropped them overboard. The likelihood of any of them being found was remote yet, remarkably, one was – by two walkers on Geilliwion Mountain, near Pontypridd.

At about 1.30 p.m. things began to happen. The balloon neared the cloud tops and the sound of breaking surf could be heard. On entering cloud the gas cooled and the rate of descent increased alarmingly and, having no ballast to drop, there was nothing that could be done to arrest it. When they emerged from the cloudbase, the three aeronauts were confronted by what they later learned to be the furnace of the Cwmafan Copper Works: 'The fire and smoke of which filled them with astonishment not to mention alarm.' They had no cause to fear that infernal scene, however, as their rate of descent was exceeded only by their groundspeed. Borne on the wings of a near gale force wind, the balloon cleared Cwmafan and struck the ground at Caerhysddu some three miles from Neath, in what Spencer later described as the roughest landing of his considerable experience – rough enough in fact to fracture Gertrude Bacon's right forearm. It rebounded high into the air and, having touched down for a second time, dragged across the mountain top for a considerable distance, its flailing grapnel acquiring several score yards of iron fencing in the process. An encounter with a barbed wire fence served only to tear the reverential trousers and severely lacerate a leg contained therein, while the next obstacle, a dead oak tree, shattered on impact, most of its branches being carried away in the balloon netting. After a few minutes the grapnel finally took hold and the balloon and its occupants, all of them somewhat the worse for wear, finally came to rest.

When help arrived in the form of the landowner, Mr W.H. Hunkin and some of his workmen, the aeronauts, none of whom had heard the Welsh language spoken before, became even more confused as to their whereabouts than they had been previously. That situation was soon rectified, however, and life at Caerhysddu began to return to normal. The balloon was packed up, a rustic labourer who, upon witnessing the spectacle had uttered a great cry of 'the Boers have come' and locked himself in a stable, was finally coaxed out, and the party of adventurers withdrew to a Neath doctor's surgery to have their various injuries attended to prior to their return to Newbury by train.

The incident was the beginning of a long association between the Bacon family and the district for John Bacon's son, Frederic, was to hold the Chair of Engineering at University College, Swansea, for many years.

The whole escapade is delightfully and succinctly summed up in this piece of cockney doggerel published in the London periodical *The Globe* shortly afterwards:

> *I'm thinking no rasher excursion's been tiken*
> *Than that meteor hunt by balloon of old Bicon.*
> *As it dived towards the earth getting nigher an'nigher,*
> *I reckon he thought, 'Ere's the fat in the fire!'*
> *And when he got chucked an' lay battered an' shiken,*
> *I bet that he felt just a bit afride Bicon!*

5
The Edwardians

The nineteenth century and the Victorian Age terminated almost simultaneously when the Queen, who had been on the throne longer than most people could remember, died at Osborne House, Isle of Wight, on 22 January 1901. She was succeeded by her eldest son, then King Edward VII, whose short reign of nine years, frequently referred to as the Edwardian Age, is considered by many, most of whom did not live through it, to have been the most graceful period in British history.

Aeronautics continued apace, with ballooning and parachuting becoming increasingly popular entertainments at outdoor events. In South Wales such entertainments were particularly popular at Carmarthen and Pontypool which fall outside the scope of this story, and Pontypridd which falls within it. The first advertising balloons made their appearance in the district at that time in the shape of four captive replicas of Boer War observation balloons. Adorned with advertisements for Hudson's Soap, they were flown by Messrs C.G. Spencer during April and May 1901 from the Crindau Gas Works Field (Newport Mon.), Roath Athletic Ground (Cardiff), The Maltsters Field (Pontypridd), and the Vetch Field (Swansea). The only passengers carried appear to have been journalists.

An athletic and cycling meeting held at the Taff Vale Park, off Broadway, Pontypridd, on Whit Monday and Tuesday, 19 and 20 May 1902, was the occasion of the county's first parachute descent of the new reign. The exhibition was organised by Messrs C.G. Spencer. The parachutist 'Miss Viola Spencer of London', in reality Miss Edith Maud Cook of Ipswich, was a twenty-three-year-old 'adopted daughter' and virtual full-time professional aeronaut who on that occasion used a solo gas balloon. Monday's ascent, her eightieth, was unremarkable except for the fact that, due to the unseasonable weather that prevailed, she experienced some difficulty in pulling the release cord due to cold hands. She freed herself eventually, landed on the slope of the Garth Mountain near Efail Isaf, and was entertained to tea by Mrs Davies, 'a dear Welsh lady', who lived nearby. The balloon was slightly damaged when it landed on the mountain top.

On Tuesday, suspended below a spare envelope, she was borne away by a brisk northerly wind and, despite releasing after only ninety seconds of flight, fell into the clutches of a tree near the Llantrisant road at Tonteg, several miles from her take-off point. The balloon landed nearby. A crowd soon assembled, a rope was produced and thrown up and over a branch and, having tied the end of it around her waist, Miss Spencer was lowered to the ground uninjured and driven back to the park and a rousing reception.

Viola Spencer reappeared by popular demand at the August Bank Holiday Sports of Pontypridd Athletic Club on Monday and Tuesday, 4 and 5 August 1902. The wind, in contrast to Whitsun, was almost calm and both descents, her 95th and 96th, uneventful, with landings on Eglwysilan Mountain on Monday and close to the famous rocking stone on Tuesday.

A more ambitious exhibition, a double parachute descent from an otherwise unmanned balloon, organised at Taff Vale Park by Messrs C.G. Spencer on 1 June 1903, had a less happy

Capt. A.E. Smith – aeronaut, balloonist and parachutist – who was seriously injured at Pontypridd on 1 June 1903. (Molly Sedgwick)

ending. The aeronauts, 'Captain Smith and the Countess S.', more prosaically known as Alfred Edwin Smith, a twenty-eight-year-old Finsbury publican and his wife, Ellen Kate Smith, ascended suspended on opposite sides of a 25,000cu.ft gas balloon at about 5.00 p.m. A light southerly wind carried them towards the town centre and, in order to descend in view of the crowd in the park, they released prior to reaching the built up area. The 'Countess S.' descended into a tree in Ynysangharad Fields from which she was duly rescued by means of a ladder. 'Captain Smith' was less fortunate, dropping onto some telephone wires that spanned the River Taff. Out of reach of a ladder or other means of rescue, he rid himself of the parachute and commenced to work his way along the wires towards the bank. All seemed to go well at first but he was unable to sustain his grip due to the wires cutting into his hands and, to the horror of the onlookers, fell some 50ft into the shallow water below sustaining injuries of so serious a nature as to necessitate a three-month stay in Cardiff Royal Infirmary. Apparently he never fully recovered for, at the inquest into his death by cyanide poisoning in April 1914, Ellen Smith laid the blame for his state of mind on the Pontypridd accident and its aftermath.

The accident did little to dampen the enthusiasm of the population of Pontypridd and district for parachuting, however. In fact, in 1904, the ranks of the parachutists were swelled by the inclusion of a well-known local eccentric, Mr C.G. Stephens, 'the Daredevil Barber of Ferndale', a man who numbered among his hobbies spending evenings in lions' cages at the local menagerie. His first descent from a Spencer-operated right away balloon was advertised to take place at the Whit Monday Sports at Taff Vale Park on 23 May. In the event rain rendered a parachute descent inadvisable so he and another local resident, Mr David Mathias, ascended as passengers in the basket of the balloon under the command of Capt. Arthur Spencer on a flight that terminated at Abergavenny.

So bad was the weather on Tuesday that the sports were postponed until Wednesday when conditions had greatly improved. The balloon was inflated and Stephens, attired in a red velvet jacket and socks and blue knickerbockers, took his seat on the rim of the basket opposite that great favourite of the Pontypridd crowd, the ever-cheerful Viola Spencer. They appeared to have attained a considerable height before Miss Spencer dropped and at least 1,000ft more before Stephens followed suit. Miss Spencer landed near Ynysybwl and Stephens on the other side of the river between Cilfynydd and Abercynon. The returned together to the park to the customary ovation.

The Daredevil Barber's exhibitionist career took a new turn on 29 December 1904 when he outpointed 'Professor' Russett of Bristol in a three round boxing contest at Gracecraft's Menagerie, Pontypridd – in a cage occupied by a lion named Wallace. All concerned survived. He returned to parachuting on 7 August 1905 when he ascended from a sports meeting at Taff Vale Park beneath a solo gas balloon and landed on the Senghenydd side of Eglwysilan Mountain. Shortly afterwards he expressed an interest in shooting Niagara Falls in a barrel. He left his Penrhiwceiber home one day in April 1906 and went missing. Whether he ever returned I know not, but he played no further part in this story.

On Whit Monday 20 May 1907 the management of the Theatre Royal, Merthyr Tydfil, organised a fête in Penydarren Park where, *The Cardiff Times* reported: 'Don Pedro walked the high wire and people in search of a mild adventure made ascents in a captive balloon.' Two days later the balloon, which it hardly needs saying belonged to Messrs C.G. Spencer, left the park in free flight and tracked in a south westerly direction. The names of its occupants and its place of landing are not recorded.

The first parachute exhibition in Cardiff since the death of Louisa Evans eleven years previously was advertised to take place at the Cardiff Boilermakers Sports and Gala at the Sophia Gardens on 5 August 1907. As the committee were unwilling to pay for an extension to the gas main the parachutist, the well-known Miss Viola Fleet of Harrow, used a hot air balloon, the inflation of which did not go according to plan. Her problems began when some of the corrugated iron sheeting covering the trench fell into the fire, thereby impeding the heating process. Eventually, however, she judged the balloon to be sufficiently buoyant to lift her weight, climbed into the parachute sling and gave the order to let go. Unfortunately one helper, a large man, did not, and continued to cling to the parachutist who failed to rise. Despite her entreaties he maintained his grip and the pair of them were dragged across the gardens towards the River Taff. Happily the balloon deflated before they reached the bank and the ascent was abandoned.

Problems dogged an attempted double ascent by one of the Spencer Brothers, whose name was not given, and an 'adopted daughter', Elsa Spencer (presumably her pseudonym), at Taff Vale Park, Pontypridd, on 8 June 1908. The problem lay in the quality of the gas with which the balloon was filled. It rose to a height of about 50ft, barely cleared the surrounding houses and drifted at rooftop level down the valley towards Treforest. Eventually it descended to within a few feet of the towpath of the Glamorgan Canal, onto which Elsa Spencer dropped. Relieved of her weight the balloon climbed rapidly to about 4,000ft from which height the captain parachuted to a landing near Taffs Well.

The following evening the couple were airborne again, that time more successfully in a right away balloon. Elsa Spencer departed the basket at 2,000ft and alighted in a field of clover on the mountainside between Glyntaff and Eglwysilan, 'about a mile from the road' she was told. 'It must have been a Welsh mile,' she remarked wryly when she finally arrived back at the sports ground. Meanwhile Capt. Spencer, finding the wind to be favourable, decided to save himself the cost of the Pontypridd to Cardiff part of the balloon's journey back to London by flying it to Cardiff. As he crossed the city he was followed by a large crowd of pedestrians who watched him valve down to a stand up landing on the east side of the Roath Basin from where the balloon was conveyed on a railway truck to Cardiff General Station.

The opposite problem to that just described beset Capt. Bidmead, the last Edwardian aeronaut to fly in the district, namely that of returning to earth. He ascended beneath his solo gas balloon *Falcon* from a fête in aid of the building fund of St Luke's Church, Canton, Cardiff, held at the Sophia Gardens, Cardiff at 7.30 p.m. on 24 June 1908. After take-off he noticed that some of his parachute lines were tangled and by the time he had managed to unravel them the balloon had reached a height of 8,000ft above Leckwith, where it appeared as a tiny speck to the spectators back at the Sophia Gardens. He dropped and landed uneventfully in a field adjoining Graves Farm near the Alps Quarry, Wenvoe. The balloon continued towards Barry where it was found in a field near Barry Dock later that night. The intrepid Bidmead promptly commandeered a bicycle and pedalled his way back to Sophia Gardens where he appeared with the parachute draped over his shoulder and made 'a pleasant little speech' to the expectant crowd.

Although ballooning continued up to and after the First World War and never died out entirely, it went into a considerable decline, eclipsed by a new, noisy and exciting form of flight – aviation. It was not until the 1960s that the most wonderful and pointless form of flight began the revival to the healthy state that it enjoys today.

A hot air balloonist ascending. No locally taken photographs seem to have survived so this one of Dolly Shepherd, an Edwardian parachutist who lived to the age of ninety-six years, has been included in order to illustrate the principles. (Molly Sedgwick)

6

The Airshipmen

It must now be obvious to the reader that free balloons are of limited utility due to their inability to travel in any other direction than that dictated by the wind. The evolution of steerable balloons, known as airships, or dirigibles – from the French *diriger*, to direct – exercised the minds of many, including a number of Cardiffians, for over fifty years before even modest success was achieved. The two major obstacles were the provision of motive power and a means of steering.

The world's first airship, constructed by the eminent French steam engineer, Henri Giffard, made its maiden flight on 24 September 1852. It consisted of a cigar-shaped balloon 144ft in length with a maximum diameter of 40ft, containing 88,300cu.ft of hydrogen from which was suspended a car that accommodated the pilot and a steam engine which, with its attendant boiler, weighed 350lb and delivered a mere 3hp. After ascending from the Paris Hippodrome, Giffard succeeded in covering a distance of seventeen miles and achieving a maximum speed of 6mph. It was the beginning of powered flight, but obviously such a slow moving aircraft could only make headway against the lightest of winds.

The unavailability of light, powerful engines hampered further progress and few of the numerous airships constructed in the ensuing fifty years, powered variously by steam, gas, electricity and even pedals, could equal the performance of Giffard's original design. It took the development of the four stroke petrol engine and the genius and courage of a Paris-domiciled Brazilian, Alberto Santos-Dumont, who between 1898 and 1901 built and flew a series of slow but fairly manageable airships, to effect any marked improvement. No significant efforts were made in Great Britain until 1902 when Stanley Spencer constructed a small airship 75ft long and 20ft diameter, powered by 3½hp Simms water-cooled petrol engine. Its maiden flight on 22 September from the Crystal Palace to Eastcote, a distance of sixteen miles, took one hour and forty minutes.

The low airspeed of early airships produced little airflow over their rudders and elevators, rendering control sluggish and imprecise. One man who believed that he had discovered the solution to the problem was Capt. William Beedle who, as will be seen, was responsible for initiating a period of significant airship activity in Cardiff between the years 1905 and 1910. A Londoner by birth, and a piano and organ builder and tuner by trade, he had spent most of his adult life in South Africa where he had gained considerable experience as an aeronaut. While so engaged he had turned his mind to the problem of airship control and had hit upon the idea of using a steering propeller to direct the bow of the craft in any given direction – vertically, horizontally or a combination of both. It was a clever concept, somewhat similar to the tail rotor of a modern helicopter but differing in that its axis of rotation could be moved through 360 degrees in order to thrust the bow to which it was fitted, in the desired direction. When no control inputs were required the propeller was declutched from the transmission and remained stationary.

He returned to his native London around the turn of the century in order to pursue his ideas and an airship incorporating them was constructed at Alexandra Palace in 1903. Its envelope 93ft long and 20ft maximum diameter, whose capacity was variously reported to be 22,000 or 26,000cu.ft, supported a 50ft long triangular sectioned framework of bicycle tubing braced by steel wire. The power unit, an 18hp, four-cylinder, water-cooled Blake petrol engine, drove via clutches and reduction gears, two propellers, one a 12ft diameter pusher mounted at the stern and the other an 8ft diameter steering propeller in the bow. A tethered trial took place at Alexandra Palace on 3 November 1903 but was not entirely successful, Beedle commenting that the front end of the frame needed considerable strengthening. Work then seems to have ceased probably due to financial constraints.

In 1904 Beedle moved to Cardiff and set up in business as a piano and organ tuner working from his home at 54 Strathnairn Street, Roath. He brought the airship with him and early in 1905, doubtless hoping to attract a financial backer, exhibited it at St Mary's Vestry Hall, now a shop premises, at 75 St Mary Street. It was probably as a result of the exhibition that he met the father and son J.T. and E.T. Willows.

Joseph Thompson Willows was a prominent citizen of Cardiff. A dental surgeon by profession, he originated from Hull but had practiced in Cardiff since 1884. A man of considerable financial means, he was a member of the executive committee of the Cardiff Musical Society and a pioneer motorist who was for many years the highly respected honorary secretary of the South Wales Automobile Club. His son, Ernest Thompson Willows, a Cardiffian by birth, had after completing his education at Clifton College, Bristol, followed him into dentistry but had displayed little enthusiasm and had terminated his training at an early stage. Beedle, it appears, fired the imagination of the mechanically minded nineteen-year-old who, in turn, seems to have had little difficulty in persuading his father to provide the financial backing required for further development. So with William Beedle's expertise, Ernest Willows' enthusiasm and Joseph Willows' capital as its major assets, The Beedle Propeller Syndicate was formed, its objectives being to design and construct a new small airship incorporating Beedle's principles and demonstrate it to the military and naval authorities in the hope of obtaining sufficient orders to enable an airship manufacturing business to be established.

The project went ahead with remarkable speed. Land was rented from Mr William Williams, Splott Farm, East Moors, chosen for its level ground and hopefully steady winds, and a wood and galvanised iron shed complete with old style sulphuric acid and iron filings gas plant constructed. The airship too took shape with great rapidity, all the work being subcontracted to local businesses. The envelope made of Japanese silk supplied by Messrs G.A. Seccombe & Co., milliners and drapers of 79-81 Queen Street, was cut and assembled by Mr Peter Hurst, tailor of 32 High Street, in a disused dance hall. All mechanical work was carried out by Messrs Hopkins, Sully & Co., motor engineers, 43A Penarth Road, while the engine – a 9hp Peugeot two-cylinder racing motorcycle engine chosen 'because nothing better was available' – was supplied by Mr John Bould, motorcycle dealer of Castle Road, Roath.

The result of their labours was the *Alexandra Airship*, a very small airship indeed, intended solely to demonstrate Beedle's principles as inexpensively as possible. Its envelope, just 70ft long and 18ft diameter, had a capacity of 12,000cu.ft, sufficient only to lift one person. The frame included a platform amidships on which the pilot stood adjacent to the engine which was air cooled by fans, drive to the propellers being by a system of shafts and chains which geared them to half engine speed. No concession was made to silence, the exhaust gases

The Alexandra Airship, *later known as the* Willows I, *at the East Moors, Cardiff 1905. Note its banana-like appearance.* (National Museums & Galleries of Wales)

merely being passed below the platform via a flexible pipe. Beedle's original steering propeller design was superceded by a twin co-axial arrangement, the single pusher at the stern remaining unaltered.

The ship was inflated around June 1905 and made its first appearance on Thursday 27 July when it was held captive while the mechanism was checked. There then ensued a lengthy wait for suitable weather and it was not until 17 August that it reappeared for what was intended to be its maiden flight. About a dozen people were present on the flying ground and a small number of interested spectators watched from the adjoining lane as it was photographed and ballasted. They were destined to be disappointed, however, as the engine refused to start and by the time the problem, a fault in the Brown & Barlow carburettor, had been traced and repaired, an hour's delay had ensued. The ship was allowed to rise, held down by a handling party of eighteen men, but a freshening wind causing flying to be abandoned for the day and it was returned to its shed.

After a further delay awaiting suitable weather the first flight took place on 15 September. The ship ascended at 3.35 p.m., with E.T. Willows at the controls, and remained airborne until after 5.00 p.m., during which time it ascended to an estimated height of 120ft, manoeuvred successfully, and demonstrated its ability to make progress in the face of a 10mph wind. Why all the flying of the *Alexandra Airship* was entrusted to Ernest Willows while the vastly more experienced Beedle remained on the ground is a mystery. One can only assume that the fact that his father held the purse strings had some bearing on the matter.

As trials progressed and lessons were learned, modifications, some quite major, were made. The shortness of the original frame and its attachment towards the centre of the envelope caused the latter to sag and take on the appearance of a banana. The problem was overcome by lengthening the frame and fitting attachment points throughout the length of the envelope. That, in turn, necessitated considerable work in lengthening the transmission. It is

E.T. Willows (inset) flying the modified Alexandra Airship, *retrospectively named the* Willows IA *airship.* (National Museums & Galleries of Wales)

uncertain when that work was carried out. E.T. Willows, interviewed in 1926, said that he thought it was done in July but he was unsure as he kept no records. As his recollection of other events proved to be suspect the information cannot be considered reliable.

Fired by their initial success, the syndicate arranged a demonstration on 11 September before an invited audience that included the Mayor and Mayoress of Cardiff (Alderman and Mrs R. Hughes). Unfortunately, as is so often the case on such occasions, things did not run smoothly. After a short time in the air one of the trail ropes caught in the transmission which rendered the airship uncontrollable. It was manhandled back to the ground where it was found that some damage had been sustained necessitating a return to the shed for repairs.

A demonstration before members of the press on 30 September was attended by greater success, a groundspeed of 15mph against a 6-7mph headwind being reportedly achieved. The final outing occurred on 20 October before Col. J.E. Capper CB, RE, the officer commanding the War Office Balloon Section, Farnborough. It is probable that on that flight the propeller arrangement was reversed with a tractor propeller for propulsion and the steering propellers at the rear. It was reported that an attempt was to be made to fly over Cardiff but in the event engine problems intervened and only a captive flight was made. Capper, however, expressed himself 'very pleased with its construction and potential utility.' Despite his praise no official interest was expressed, no orders were forthcoming and the *Alexandra Airship* was deflated in November. Although it remained in existence for at least another three and a half years, it never flew again.

Beedle and the Willows' continued to collaborate in airship design and construction for a number of years after then, although their dreams of becoming airship manufacturers were somewhat diminished. They appear to have abandoned the idea of the steering propeller and concentrated instead on producing a system of propellers that could, in addition to producing forward thrust, be swivelled to produce lift and control the airship in the vertical plane – an early example of vectored thrust that is still used on modern airships. Beedle and Willows senior continued their musical and dental careers whilst Willows junior became the Cardiff agent for the Fairbanks Motor Co., working from an office in Premier Buildings, 6-7 St John's Street, Cardiff, which was also given as the address of the Beedle Propeller Syndicate. In 1906 they produced two airship frames conforming to the new design philosophy that were never flown. By 1908 they had constructed a new airship, powered by an unspecified four-cylinder water-cooled engine that was nearing inflation and trials when its nacelle was purchased by the War Office Balloon Factory at Farnborough, 'which from facts since revealed were obtained solely for the purpose of guiding them in the system of swivelling propellers brought out on the Army Airship *Delta*', wrote a bitter E.T. Willows many years later.

Shortly afterwards Beedle and the Willows' parted company, almost certainly acrimoniously although the reason is unknown. Beedle moved to Watford, Hertfordshire, where in 1909 the Beedle Propeller & Aeroplane Co. Ltd was established by two local entrepreneurs, its stated objectives being 'to acquire the interests of W. Beedle and the Beedle Propeller Syndicate in patent rights in connection with propellers for ships, aeroplanes and dirigible balloons, etc.' The company achieved little success.

Ernest Willows was never to mention William Beedle's name publicly again. Retrospectively he invariably referred to the *Alexandra Airship* as the *Willows I* or *Willows IA*, depending on its modification state, and, in the numerous interviews and articles that he subsequently gave and wrote, he always conveyed the impression that it was entirely the work of his father and himself. Beedle. for his part, made no effort to contradict Willows' statements. He continued to live modestly in Watford tuning pianos and, I am told, dabbling in the design of air conditioning fans until his death on 4 October 1931 at the age of seventy-two.

During the period when the local airship fraternity was confined to the ground, the skies of Glamorgan were traversed by a somewhat bizarre aerial visitant in the form of the French military airship *Patrie*. A Lebaudy Airship, generally considered to be the first truly practical airship design, she was a large craft for her day. Her semi-rigid envelope, that is one incorporating a rigid keel at its base to impart added strength, contained 114,800cu.ft of hydrogen. She left her base at Verdun at the Franco-German border on Friday 29 November 1907, her complement augmented by the presence of two generals intent on obtaining an aerial view of the border fortifications. However, a problem with her 70hp Panhard et Levassor engine necessitated an unscheduled landing at Souhesmes, some 14km from Verdun, where the passengers and crew disembarked while work was carried out on the engine and the large amount of gas valved during the descent replaced. It was at that point that the wind got up! A sudden squall took hold of *Patrie*, who, like a large wayward dog, dragged her handling party of some 200 soldiers across the landing field and into a hedge where, in a scene that would have put the Keystone Cops to shame, they were obliged to let go the handling lines. Her horrified captain and crew could only watch helplessly as their charge rose unmanned to an enormous height and disappeared in a north-westerly direction, no doubt reappraising their career aspirations as they did so.

The airship's fate remained a matter for speculation until 7.00 a.m. on Sunday 1 December when a large, yellow, fishlike object became dimly discernible in the sky above Swansea and district, having presumably drifted along the Glamorgan coast under cover of darkness. She left Glamorgan airspace at sunrise, flew low over Llanelli, then adopted a more northerly

3. — VERDUN. Le Dirigeable " *Patrie* ". - Les préparatifs pour son ascension du 29 novembre 1907.

The French military airship Patrie *being prepared for her ill-fated flight of 29 November 1907.* (Ventry Collection, care of the Airship Heritage Trust)

track that took her up the Gwendraeth Valley at which point the rising sun warmed her gas causing her to ascend to a greater altitude. For the remainder of that morning the peregrinations of the errant aerostat were a source of wonderment to the populace of Carmarthenshire and Cardiganshire until she was finally lost to view when high over Cardigan Bay.

At a little after 4.00 p.m. she made landfall over the coast of County Antrim, Northern Ireland, her buoyancy by then adversely affected by the cooling evening air. She came to earth near the village of Ballysallagh where she ploughed two large furrows as she dragged across the ground, depositing in the process several hundredweight of mechanical components whose loss lightened her sufficiently to rise again into the darkening skies and resume her north westerly progress towards the Atlantic. She was never seen again!

Following Beedle's departure, E.T. Willows continued his airship work alone, although in March 1909 he did team up briefly with one D.M. Bowyer-Smyth of Cardiff, an enthusiast of flapping and rotary wing flight, to form The Welsh Aero Club, whose address was also at Premier Buildings, St John Street, an organisation that came to little. The same month be also exhibited the envelope of the *Alexandra Airship* at the Society of Motor Manufacturers & Traders first Aero Exhibition held at Olympia between 19 and 27 March. From a photograph it appears that the frame and mechanism had been removed, presumably because William Beedle held the patent rights.

Later in the year another Willows airship appeared. Known as the *Willows II*, it was constructed to the design philosophy that was to characterise all future Willows airships. How much credit for that philosophy is due to Willows and how much to Beedle it is impossible to be sure but it does appear that the design owed much to the combined efforts of the two men during the period 1906-1908. The steering propeller was abandoned in favour of a conventional rudder. Two propellers mounted one each side of the car faced forward for normal

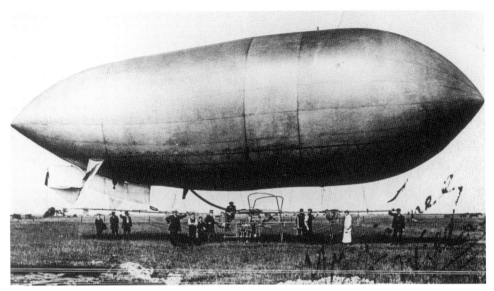

The Willows II *airship.* (National Museums & Galleries of Wales)

flight but could be swivelled by means of a system of bevel gears to produce a down thrust that controlled the ship in the vertical plane thereby obviating the need for elevators.

As before, all work was sub-contracted, the mechanical components again being entrusted to Messrs Hopkins, Sully & Co. The envelope, purchased 'off the shelf' from Messrs C.G. Spencer, was one of a series of identical examples produced by them at the time. Larger and more sophisticated than that of the *Alexandra Airship*, it was 86ft long, 22ft diameter and of 21,000cu.ft capacity. It was fitted with a top gas valve, automatic gas and air valves and a ripping panel. A one tenth capacity ballonet occupied the centre of the lower half. Below the envelope was fitted a 58ft boom constructed from 3in bamboo and 3in steel tube, to which was attached the 10ft-long triangular-sectioned car built of steel tube that contained the engine, its four gallon fuel tank and the pilot's seat. That authoritative tome *Jane's All The World's Airships (Aeroplanes and Dirigibles) 1909* gives the engine as a 20hp Curtiss but in the event the ship was fitted with a 30hp J.A.P. V8 acquired secondhand from Mr J.E. Humphreys, another air-minded dentist, who had installed it in his Wyvenhoe Flier, the first, albeit totally unsuccessful, flying boat built in Great Britain. The increased size of the new airship necessitated an increase in size of Willow's shed, the increased height being compensated for by digging a trench in the floor.

The maiden flight took place on 26 November 1909 when the airship rose to a height of about 200ft and manoeuvred successfully. Further flights took place on 5, 8 and 18 December; on the latter occasion Willows remained aloft for an hour and a quarter before the Lord Mayor (Cllr John Chappel JP) and other local dignitaries. Willows pronounced himself satisfied with the trials and the airship was deflated. During the winter months the mechanism was overhauled, new 6ft Handley Page propellers fitted in place of the original crude stop-gap examples, the boom replaced by an improved design and the envelope re-varnished.

In June 1910 the envelope was re-inflated using bottles of compressed hydrogen for the first time, thereby reducing inflation time from three days to four hours. After a number of further trials, during which he assessed the speed of the ship to be 16mph and its rate of climb to be 1,000ft per minute, Ernest Willows was at last ready to leave the environs of East Moors and embark upon a series of flights that in the course of just six months were to transform him from a virtual unknown to an international celebrity.

Early in 1910 a group of prominent citizens, the Earl of Plymouth, Lord Ninian Crichton-Stuart, Viscount Tredegar, Lord Aberdare, Sir W.T. Lewis and Mr D.A. Thomas MP, offered a prize of £50 to the first airman to fly over Cardiff. It was clearly intended as an encouragement to Willows who clearly intended to win it.

The successful attempt was made in the morning of Saturday 4 June. There was virtually no wind when Willows ascended from East Moors at 6.50 a.m., rose to a height of 300ft and set course for the city centre. It was on that first flight away from base that his greatest weakness as a flier became apparent for the first time. His ability as a navigator was minimal. In an article written in the magazine *Aeronautics* in May 1914 he confessed that he had been unable to recognise the streets and railway lines of his own home city and had the City Hall not been such a distinctive building he would have become totally lost. He reached the City Hall after a flight of seven minutes and after circling the clock tower, touched down on the grass adjacent to the recently unveiled statue of Lord Tredegar. Despite the early hour a crowd soon assembled to applaud the airman and a collection in aid of the funds of Cardiff Royal Infirmary raised over £1 0s 0d. After remaining a short time on the ground he returned to East Moors. An attempted repeat performance at 4.30 p.m. was thwarted when a broken propeller shaft obliged him to lower his trailrope and be ignominiously towed back to The Moors.

The repeat performance finally took place on Tuesday 7 June. He ascended to 500ft and routed along Newport Road, Queen Street and Duke Street to Cardiff Castle, dropping messages addressed to the Lord Mayor and the editor of the *South Wales Daily News* en route. He then turned towards Cathays Park and landed in the gardens adjacent to University College where a large crowd including the Lord Mayor and Willows' proud parents soon assembled. The £50 prize had been well and truly won and, after the sort of speeches customary on such occasions, the aeronaut took his leave and returned to base. The two messages had landed on the roof of Messrs Cox & Sons Café, Queen Street, on the site now occupied by the Capitol Shopping Centre and were delivered to the addressees by the manager Mr P.L. Baby. The Lord Mayor was in a position to express his congratulations to the aeronaut in person while the editor of the *South Wales Daily News* elected to do so by telegram only to receive the following communication from the postmaster 'I beg to inform you that the telegram handed in at the Cardiff Office addressed to Mr E.T. Willows, airman, Cathays Park, has not been delivered for the reason stated below – "Airship Flown."' However the telegram eventually reached its intended recipient.

On Saturday 18 June the *Willows II* carried its first and only passenger and nearly came to grief as a consequence. Willows had been booked to appear at a gymkhana and took with him his cousin Frank Garrett who became the first passenger to fly in an airship or powered aircraft in South Wales. They left East Moors at 5.00 p.m. but suffered a partial power failure en route. On passing low over Roath Park the cooler air above the lake cooled the airship's gas and caused a loss of lift. Never having experienced the phenomenon before Willows

E.T. Willows in the Willows II *over Roath Park Lake, Cardiff, 13 July 1910.* (Author's collection)

imagined that the envelope had developed a leak and an anxious few minutes ensued. Despite swivelling his propellers to give maximum down thrust and using all available power he was unable to arrest the descent. The jettisoning of Garrett's coat and shoes did little to alleviate the situation and the craft came to earth, happily fairly gently, on a building site near Maindy Barracks. It was manhandled into the barracks by a party of soldiers and Willows was able to inspect the envelope from a rooftop and satisfy himself that it was undamaged. Extra hydrogen to top up the envelope did not arrive until dusk so the airship was left moored in the barracks for the night. Willows returned at 4.00 a.m. to fly it out only to find the area shrouded in fog. The fog lifted somewhat at 5.00 a.m. and he unwisely elected to ascend. He rose to about 200ft, circled the barracks and set course for Penylan Observatory, the only object projecting above the fog. He climbed to 400ft where he lost all contact with the ground and spent twenty minutes completely lost. Eventually he caught sight of Rumney Hill and the Dowlais Steelworks and, groping his way through the mist finally located his landing ground.

In July the ship was deflated and transported to Montpellier Gardens, Cheltenham, where it was re-inflated and exhibited as the principal attraction at Cheltenham Carnival. It made a brief flight on Saturday 9 July and remained as a static exhibit until the evening of Monday 11 July when Willows decided that weather conditions were ideal for his next intended exploit, a prolonged cross-country flight. He elected to fly the ship back to Cardiff.

At 7.55 p.m., the wind having dropped, he ascended with an extra two gallons of petrol in a can hanging from one of the stays. He set course for Dean's Close School where he circled the playing fields in order to fulfill a promise, flew on to Gloucester where he circled the cathedral before climbing to 300ft and followed the north bank of the Severn. At Lydney he discovered his father, who had set off in advance by motor car, broken down in a farmyard. He descended to 100ft and with the aid of his megaphone was able to tell him to leave the yard and look out for the following cars. As a result he was able to obtain a lift and arrive in Cardiff in time to witness his son's arrival!

Shortly afterwards, notwithstanding the fact they he was flying along one of the easiest routes in the country from a navigational standpoint, he became uncertain of his position and had to resort to following the setting moon. Soon, however, he sighted the lights of

The Willows III *airship in which Willows and F.W. Gooden made the first airship crossing from England to France.* (Campbell McCutcheon)

Chepstow and after climbing to 600ft, the lights of Newport also. The moon then set but by then he was able to see the tipping of molten slag from the Dowlais Steelworks which led him towards his landing ground where he was guided to his shed by an acetylene lamp. He dropped his trailrope and the ship was finally docked at 11.40 p.m., having covered fifty-three miles in three hours forty-five minutes.

A further outing followed on the evening of Wednesday 13 July. Willows had been booked to appear at a YMCA carnival at Roath Park. He ascended at a little before 8.15 p.m. and flew initially to Cardiff Arms Park, which was not the built-up area it is today, where he landed to the applause of a group of cricketers at net practice. His object was to attempt a meeting with Gen. F.C. Heath RE, CB, Inspector of Royal Engineers, who was due to inspect the Glamorgan (Fortress) Royal Engineers at the park that evening. Willows waited for some time but the officer did not appear, possibly a political decision on his part, so Willows continued his journey to Roath Park where he descended over the lake and moored to a boat. He received an enthusiastic welcome and, after a wait of about twenty minutes, ascended and manoeuvred above the heads of the 16,000 strong crowd before setting course for base at about 9.30 p.m.

Willows' triumphs were the only bright spots in one of the blackest weeks in flying history up to that time. Tragedy struck first at the Bournemouth Aviation Meeting on Tuesday 10 July when the Hon. C.S. Rolls of Monmouth was killed when his modified Wright biplane suffered a structural failure in flight. The following day the well-known German sporting balloonist and airship pioneer Oskar Erbsloh died along with his four crew members in the wreckage of his airship which crashed near Düsseldorf. The final blow came on Thursday 14 when news was received that the darling of the Pontypridd crowds, Viola

Spencer, had died in the Coventry and Warwickshire Hospital from injuries received in a parachuting accident on the previous Saturday. Becalmed over the city she had released successfully and landed on a factory roof only to be dragged off it when the still inflated canopy was caught by one of the few gusts of wind of the afternoon. She had recently taken flying lessons at the Grahame-White Aviation School at Pau and claimed, almost certainly correctly, to have been the first British woman to have flown solo in an aeroplane. In contrast to that of Louisa Evans, her funeral was the subject of little public interest and she lies to this day in an unmarked grave in London Road Cemetery, Coventry. She was thirty-two years old.

Undeterred by the tragedies, Ernest Willows made plans for his next adventure, a flight from Cardiff to the Crystal Palace, London. Among his backers was a young Cardiff ship owner and entrepreneur, Samuel Einstein, a man that the flying world was to see a great deal more of.

The flight was not without its setbacks. Planned departures on 4 and 5 August had to be abandoned due to mechanical problems and vandalism respectively and it was not until 6 August 1910 that Willows, aided by a following westerly wind, finally left East Moors at 8.35 p.m. on what was destined to be the last flight of a Willows Airship from Cardiff.

He flew directly towards Bristol, thereby becoming the first person to cross the Bristol Channel in a powered aircraft, and was overhead the Cumberland Basin at 9.15 p.m. where passengers on the pleasure steamer *Barry*, about to depart for Cardiff, greeted him with loud applause and cries of 'Good old Willows! Good old Cardiff'. It was at that point he made the error of throwing out his sandwiches in mistake for ballast. The airship had by that time been fitted with a compass but as it had not been swung he planned to follow the route of the A4 to Reading where he was to rendezvous with his father and two mechanics who had preceded him by car carrying an extra fuel supply.

In all he stopped his engine about twelve times in order to ask the way from astonished citizens of various places who heard his disembodied voice from the darkness above. On one such occasion, near Newbury, he left his hard seat and sat on the propeller guard for a rest. Despite his erratic progress he outpaced the car and, despite circling Reading to await its arrival the planned rendezvous did not take place and he continued towards his destination nursing such fuel as remained.

At Esher, acting on the advice of a railway worker, he followed the London & South Western line but when within five miles of his goal his fuel supply became exhausted. The airship then became a free balloon, incapable of being steered or controlled by its propellers. Tantalisingly he passed within 200 yards of his intended destination where he threw out his grapnel which caught in a tree and snapped off. He drifted on over Sydenham, Catford and Hither Green to Mottingham where he valved gas and descended. His trail rope hit the roof of the cottage of the caretaker of the Winn Estate whose occupant emerged and, with the aid of a gang of railwaymen coming off night shift, took hold of it and brought the ship safely to earth at 6.15 a.m., it having covered the greatest distance by an airship in Great Britain up to that time.

The *Willows II* was put on exhibition, entrance to the field being 6d per person. So great was the public interest that police had to be in attendance to control the crowds. After refuelling and replenishing his gas supply Willows left on 8 August for the Crystal Palace, covering the four miles in less than ten minutes. The ship was flown several times from the Crystal

Palace, on one occasion circling St Paul's Cathedral. Willows then set about the construction of the *Willows III*, a larger ship of 32,000cu.ft, which incorporated the engine and some of the mechanism of the *Willows II*, in which he and fellow Welshman F.W. Gooden completed an epic flight from Wormwood Scrubs to Corbeheim, near Douai, during the night of 4/5 November 1910, the first airship crossing from England to France. After many trials and tribulations they reached their planned destination, Issy-les-Moulineaux, Paris, on 28 December 1910.

Ernest Willows became an international celebrity but, although he found fame, fortune always evaded him. He based himself in the English Midlands for reasons known only to himself and formed E.T. Willows Ltd – a private company to acquire his aeronautical business interests. It carried out a small amount of work but soon foundered and Willows was declared personally bankrupt in January 1913. The last vestige of his Cardiff activities, his airship shed, was sold by auction on 11 February 1913. It fetched £12 5s 0d.

The Willows Aircraft Co. was subsequently founded in Cardiff by J.T. Willows, but its activities and those of E.T. Willows were confined to the London area. He subsequently worked on airship design with Mr George Holt-Thomas' company, Airships Ltd, and was responsible for the design of three more airships – the *Willows IV*, *V* and *VI*. There is a commonly held belief, quite untrue as it happens, that he was responsible for the design of the SS Blimps used for coastal patrol work during the First World War. It stems from the fact that the first SS airship was produced by Royal Naval Air Service personnel who attached the fuselage of a B.E.2c aeroplane to the envelope of the *Willows IV*, which was renamed the *SS-1*. The *Willows VI* designed as a contender for the SS airship specification was designated *SS-2* but proved to be unsuccessful. He was commissioned as a lieutenant in the Aeronautical Inspection Department of the Royal Flying Corps from 1916–1918 working on barrage balloons and their aprons. Again popular myth, which has no foundation in fact, has credited him with the design of the system. He returned to Cardiff, and therefore to this story in 1918.

All that remains of Willows' airships today is the V8 J.A.P. engine of the *Willows II* and *III* which is displayed at the museum of the Shuttleworth Trust, Old Warden, Bedfordshire.

7
The Aviators

Heavier-than-air flight, or aviation to give it its correct name, originated with the evolution of the kite in China many years before the birth of Christ. Kites were introduced to Europe by travellers from the Orient at the time of the Renaissance and it is surprising that the idea of using them as the basis for experiment in manned flight did not occur to the would-be fliers of the time. Instead, for many centuries attempts at flight were confined to the activities of jumpers, those courageous optimists, who, with wings or other devices attached to their persons, stepped into space from high places and whose contribution to science, if any, lay solely in the field of orthopaedic surgery.

It was not until the early years of the nineteenth century that serious scientific thought began to be applied to aviation. During the ensuing hundred years numerous individuals contributed to the stock of knowledge that paved the way to practical aviation, and by the latter decades of the century gliders evolved from the principles of the kite had been flown in various parts of the world and several primitive steam-powered aircraft had puffed and lurched into the air on what can be described as very brief flights. As in the case of airships the steam engine was far too heavy for aviation purposes and it was the advent of the four stroke petrol engine that brought about the long-awaited breakthrough. Its marriage to the glider led to the birth of the aeroplane.

Who deserves credit for making the first powered heavier-than-air flight is a matter for debate and controversy frequently surrounds claims to have been the first to fly in particular countries. It all hinges on how the word 'flight' is interpreted. It is generally held, however, that the first self-sustained controlled flight by an aeroplane took place at Kitty Hawk, North Carolina, on 17 December 1903. For the pilot, Orville Wright, his brother Wilbur, and their friend and collaborator, Octave Chanute, it was the culmination of many years of painstaking research in laboratory, workshop and airborne in the various gliders they had built and flown. In the course of the following five years they improved considerably on their original design but, anxious to avoid assisting potential imitators, kept details of their progress largely to themselves with the result that reports of their activities were received with scepticism in many quarters.

European progress was slow by comparison, the first successful flights being made by Alberto Santos-Dumont near Paris in 1906, the greatest distance covered being 720ft. Controversy surrounds claims to have been the first aviator to fly in Great Britain, suffice it to say that both A.V. Roe and the American S.F. Cody made short hops in 1908 at a time when the European distance record stood at twelve miles. All concerned were given cause to reappraise their achievements later that year when Wilbur Wright visited Le Mans with a Wright A biplane and between August and December made a series of flights that amazed the onlookers with his mastery of the machine. He brought his year's work to a conclusion on 31 December by covering a distance of seventy-seven miles in two hours and twenty minutes.

Spurred on by the Wright's example European aviation began a rapid advance exemplified on 25 July 1909 by the arrival near Dover of a French motor car accessory manufacturer by the name of Louis Blériot, piloting his Blériot XI monoplane having flown from Les Baraques near Calais. The feat earned Blériot the Daily Mail Prize of £1,000 for the first crossing of the English Channel by aeroplane, a permanent place in the aviation hall of fame and, most importantly, as will become evident from the following pages, established him as one of the world's premier aeroplane manufacturers. Blériot monoplanes of the type XI, together with variants of similar appearance having more powerful engines, two seats or increased manoeuvrability formed the backbone of European aviation from 1909 until the early days of the First World War.

As the number of aviators and aeroplanes increased, national aero clubs began to issue aviator's certificates to those able to pass tests of flying proficiency, and to organise aviation meetings. The first such meeting, 'The Great Aviation Week of Champagne' was held at Rheims between 22-29 August 1909. The first British meetings were held at Blackpool and Doncaster during the following October and the British aviation sporting calendar for 1910 included proposed meetings at Doncaster, Huntingdon, Wolverhampton, Bournemouth, Lanark and Cardiff.

The Cardiff meeting was scheduled to take place at Ely Racecourse, part of which now comprises Trelai Park, between 24-27 August 1910. A company with a capital of £2,600 was formed to organise the event under an executive committee comprised of such distinguished citizens as: Lord Ninian Chrichton-Stuart; the Lord Mayor (Alderman Lewis Morgan); Capt J. Hughes-Morgan JP; Dr E.H. Griffiths, principal of the University College, Cardiff; J.T. Willows; and the well-known motoring and sailing enthusiast, Dr E. Tennison-Collins. A public appeal to raise a prize fund of £3,000 was launched but in July it was announced that the meeting had been postponed 'due to local difficulties', probably a dispute between officials of the Royal Aero Club, under whose supervision the event was to have been run, and Cardiff Corporation the owners of the land, over the need to fell some trees as a safety measure. The disagreement was not resolved, the trees remained and the meeting was abandoned.

As a result the distinction of being the first aviator to fly in the county went not to one of the great names of early aviation, but to a local man, Swansea motor trader Ernest Frank Sutton.

Ernie Sutton, as he was generally known, a partner with his brother, George Leslie Andrew Sutton, in the firm of Sutton Bros, motor engineers of Dillwyn Street, Swansea, had, in common with many young men of the day, developed a passionate interest in aviation but, unlike the majority who were content merely to read and watch, resolved to become an active aviator. To that end, in December 1910, he purchased a Blériot XI monoplane identical to that in which its designer had made the historic Channel crossing the previous year. The little monoplane had a wingspan of 28ft, a length of 25ft, an all up weight of 715lb, and was powered by a none too reliable Anzani three-cylinder air cooled engine capable of developing about 25hp on a good day.

In order to recoup some of his outlay Sutton exhibited the aeroplane at 32 Castle Street, Swansea, during the early part of 1911, charging threepence per head admission. It also featured as the main exhibit at the Conversazione and Dance of the Royal Institution of South Wales held at Swansea on 17 January 1911.

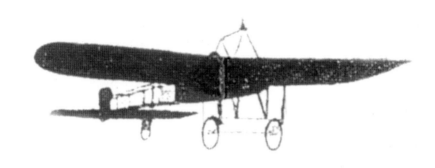

Probably the first photograph of an aeroplane in flight to be taken in South Wales. Ernest Sutton flying his Blériot XI at Oxwich Bay, Gower, on 23 January 1911.

In the meantime a hangar to house the machine had been constructed among the sand hills at the western end of Oxwich Bay, Gower, Sutton's chosen flying ground and, on 19 January the Blériot, with its wings removed, was towed by a motor car from Swansea to Oxwich. It was then manhandled with some difficulty over the sand hills onto the beach and reassembled in readiness for the first attempt at flight.

At 2.45 p.m. the engine was started and Sutton, watched by a crowd comprised of about twenty Swansea people and a considerable number of fascinated locals, taxied the length of the beach, turned the aeroplane round and returned to Oxwich. Evidently satisfied with his progress he then decided to attempt his first flight. A light wind blew across the beach from the landward side so he taxied the Blériot to the water's edge, turned into the wind and applied full power. After a short run the machine became airborne on what was of necessity a short hop due to the limited space available, and landed successfully having made the first heavier-than-air flight in the county. Onlookers estimated the distance flown to have been approximately 100 yards and the height attained 20ft. He repeated the feat several times before the onset of darkness obliged him to hangar the machine.

It reappeared on 23 January when Sutton embarked upon a series of increasingly ambitious flights until a minor disaster struck. He commenced with a flight from a spot near his hangar towards High Tor during which he remained airborne for about a mile and reached an estimated height of 50ft. Having landed successfully, he turned the machine around, took off again and returned to Oxwich. On his third flight, a return to High Tor, he climbed to about 150ft and yet again landed successfully, remarkable progress for one of so little experience. His inexperience and undoubted overconfidence proved, quite literally, to be his downfall on his fourth flight when he climbed too steeply after take-off and the low-powered Blériot stalled and nose-dived onto the beach shattering the propeller and severely damaging the engine bearers and undercarriage. Sutton escaped with no more than a grazed arm and a skinned index finger. Despite the setback he seemed well pleased with his progress and reportedly sang as he dismantled the damaged aeroplane prior to conveying it back to its hangar. After repairs and a wait for suitable weather, he recommenced flying on 6 March. After a series of short hops he attempted a longer flight only to crash sustaining similar damage as before. The Blériot was soon made airworthy again and throughout the long, hot summer notable for its bathing tragedies, industrial unrest and the Coronation of His Majesty King George V, Ernie Sutton flew frequently, displaying increasing confidence and skill. By the end of May he had mastered the art of turning, made a flight of two and a half miles and reached a height of 200ft.

Like the balloon and parachute before it the aeroplane soon became an object of popular entertainment, the majority of early aviators being showmen who toured the country giving aerial exhibitions to an enthralled public. An early and spectacularly unsuccessful practitioner of the display pilot's art was Capt. Cecil Clayton who was engaged to appear at the Bridgend Fête and Gala at Trews Field off Tondu Road on 6 June 1911, the first public flying display in the county. Clayton was essentially an entertainer. The manager of the Grand Theatre, Mansfield, Nottinghamshire, he was also an aeronaut and veteran of some 300 parachute descents over the previous sixteen years. Quick to visualise the potential of

Advertisement for the first aeroplane exhibition in South Wales by Cecil Clayton on 6 June 1911.

the aeroplane as a lucrative crowd puller, he had enrolled as a pupil at the Blériot flying school at Pau but had made poor progress and left without gaining an aviator's certificate. However, as the lack of a certificate was no bar to piloting an aeroplane at the time, he purchased a Blériot XI and attempted to teach himself to fly in the vicinity of Mansfield.

The Blériot's first public appearance on 9 June 1910 was, if nothing else, eventful. Piloted by an equally inept associate of Clayton, a circus trick cyclist called Beresford, it ploughed into a badly controlled crowd at the Hereford and Worcester Agricultural Show at Worcester Racecourse, leaving a woman spectator dead and five other people injured. Despite being severely censured Clayton continued with his aviational ambitions and almost exactly a year later he and the Blériot arrived at Bridgend by train.

He made a short hop to test the machine in the evening of Monday 5 June and, true to form, overran into the fence and damaged the propeller. On Tuesday a crowd of 3,000 people assembled to witness the exhibition. Whether they received their moneys worth rather depended on what they had hoped to see. At 6.00 p.m. the aviator took his seat, the engine was started and shortly afterwards the Blériot commenced its take off run. It failed to rise but on that occasion Clayton managed to bring it to a standstill before hitting the fence and taxied back to the starting point. On his second attempt he became airborne after a run of some thirty yards and crossed the fence at a height of about 20ft but for some inexplicable reason failed to gain further height and found himself confronted by a mill. In an attempt to avoid the building he turned left but in so doing allowed the nose of the aeroplane to drop with the result that it dived into the ground with a splintering crash. Clayton emerged from the wreckage unscathed but the débâcle appears to have finally convinced him that aviation was not his forté and his future aerial activities were confined to the field of aeronautics.

In contrast, at Oxwich, Ernest Sutton continued to make steady progress and by September was reaching heights of 400ft and remained airborne on one occasion for a period of seven minutes. That same month a man who was destined to become one of the legendary figures of early British aviation demonstrated to the citizens of Cardiff just how far it had advanced in its first three years – and made a little history in so doing. His name was B.C. Hucks.

Bentfield Charles Hucks, Benny to his friends, was no stranger to Cardiff. Born at Stansted, Essex, in 1884 he had, after completing engineering training with Messrs Thorneycroft at Basingstoke, held a number of positions in the motor trade culminating in his appointment as head tester and demonstrator with The Automobile Co. of 20 Charles Street, Cardiff. His motor career was abruptly cut short in the Cardiff Magistrates Court in 1909 when he was fined £50 and banned from driving for three years for travelling along Queen Street at the breakneck speed of 14mph. Seeking a new direction in which to apply his engineering skills, he found employment as a mechanic with the British aviation pioneer Claude Grahame-White and accompanied him on his United States tour of 1910. On returning to England he joined the young Robert Blackburn, a pioneer British aircraft constructor at Filey, Yorkshire, taught himself to fly and was awarded Royal Aero Club Aviators Certificate, No.91, on 30 May 1911.

During the late summer of 1911, the Blackburn Co., of which Hucks had become chief test pilot, embarked upon a demonstration tour of the West Country. Commencing at Taunton on August Bank Holiday Monday and proceeding in the course of the following weeks to Burnham, Minehead and Weston-super-Mare, Hucks gave numerous displays in a

Blackburn Mercury monoplane powered by a 50hp Gnome seven-cylinder rotary engine, considered by many to be the first reliable aero engine ever produced.

While appearing at Weston-super-Mare at the end of August, Hucks announced his intention of attempting a flight across the Bristol Channel to Cardiff, a promise he kept on the morning of 1 September 1911. Taking advantage of light early morning winds he donned a lifejacket and took off from his flying ground at Locking at 5.10 a.m., climbed to 1,500ft and set course for Cardiff where he circled the City Hall, dropping messages addressed to the editors of local newspapers as he did so. He then made a wide sweep over Llanishen, Whitchurch, Gabalfa and Llandaff, before commencing the return journey to Weston. As he coasted out in the vicinity of Roath Dock all work came to a standstill as dockers gazed in awe at the monoplane, its high aspect ratio wings illuminated by the rays of the rising sun, giving it the appearance of an enormous dragonfly. The return crossing was completed without incident and Hucks touched down at Locking at 5.50 a.m. having become the first aviator to cross the Bristol Channel.

Having concluded the programme of displays at Weston it was decided to continue what was developing into a highly successful and lucrative tour to include Cardiff and so, at 5.45 a.m. on 10 September, Hucks set off on his second Bristol Channel crossing. At the time a number of aviators were operating The Coronation Aerial Post, a mail service between Hendon and Windsor, the first occasion that mail had been conveyed by aeroplane in the United Kingdom, and at the request of Mr R.C. Tombs ISO, a member of the honorary committee of the Coronation Aerial Post, Hucks too carried a letter from him addressed to Mr T.S. Fairgray, the Head Postmaster at Cardiff.

After crossing the Channel Hucks made his landfall near the mouth of the River Taff and followed the river and North Road inland until, he claimed, he spotted a large field that appeared to afford a suitable landing place. He touched down after a flight of sixteen and a half minutes on the turf of the Cardiff and County Polo Club ground at Whitchurch, a site now covered by housing to the rear of the Three Arches public house.

Hucks' claim that his choice of landing field was entirely fortuitous seemed to be stretching credulity a little far when he disclosed that, by sheer coincidence, he was met by an old friend from his Cardiff motoring days, Mr G.H. Henshaw, who happened to be strolling on the polo ground at 6 o'clock on a Sunday morning! Whatever the truth of the matter the landing subsequently led to some acrimonious correspondence between the assistant secretary of the polo club and Hucks who remained unabashed.

The monoplane's wings were subsequently removed and it was wheeled to the Cardiff Tramways sheds at Llandaff where it remained until the following day when it was transported to the American Roller Skating Rink in Westgate Street, situated near the present south entrance of the Millennium Stadium, where it was put on public exhibition. The Blackburn remained on exhibition for over a week, with Hucks on hand to explain its workings, until negotiations had been completed with Cardiff Corporation and the Cardiff Race Club for the hire of Ely Racecourse as the venue for a week of exhibition flying. Agreement was reached and the first exhibition was arranged for 21 September. It marked the beginning of aerial activity at Ely Racecourse that was to continue intermittently for over forty years.

A large crowd paid an admission charge of 1s, with children at half price, to witness the aviator in action and by all accounts they were not disappointed. In the face of a gusty westerly wind he took off early in the afternoon and flew a wide circuit encompassing Tumble Hill, Leckwith and Sloper Road before touching down to much applause at his starting point. During the course of the afternoon he made several more flights, on one occasion flying over Penarth Dock.

The following morning it came to Hucks' notice that rumours were circulating in the locality to the effect that he was not proposing to give any further exhibitions. In order to dispel them he took off at 12.10 p.m. and made a twenty-five minute flight over the city distributing handbills from a height of 2,000ft. The flight certainly appeared to have made a lasting impression on at least one local resident for on the following Monday morning the Cardiff Coroner, Mr W.L. Yorath, was told that James Robert White, a blacksmith of King's Road, Canton, who was sitting down to his midday meal, had exclaimed to his wife, 'I think I can hear that aeroplane' – and dropped dead over the dining table. Medical evidence gave the cause of death as 'syncope brought about by excitement and the process of digestion.' Hucks flew several times that afternoon and evening continuing until dusk.

There then arrived on the scene one Harry Grindell-Matthews, a thirty-one-year-old electrical engineer. A native of Winterbourne near Bristol he had, after service in the Boer War, embarked on a career in what would now be called electronics and had developed and patented an early form of radio telephone known as the 'Aerophone'. With the aid of a number of backers he had formed the Grindell-Matthews Wireless Telephone Co. Ltd, and had for some time been conducting tests across the Severn Estuary from a base at Chepstow. On hearing that Hucks was in the locality his thoughts turned towards trying out his apparatus in the air and he approached the aviator who readily agreed to co-operate.

On Saturday 23 September aerials were attached to the Blackburn and the experiments began. Unfortunately only one transmitter was serviceable which was retained by Grindell-Matthews on the ground, Hucks being provided with a receiver and headphones in the aeroplane. After successful ground tests first with the engine stationary, then with it running, the aviator took off on that wet and blustery afternoon to continue the experiment aloft. History was made as Hucks crossed the racecourse flying at 85mph at 700ft travelling in the direction of St Fagans when he heard through his headphones above the noise of the engine and slipstream Grindell-Matthews' voice calling, 'Hello! Hello!' It was claimed to be the first time that a human voice, as opposed to Morse code, had been transmitted to an aircraft in flight and, despite considerable research, I have discovered no earlier claim. It was fascinating to reflect as I sat in the flightdeck of a modern airliner in the skies above Europe listening to the continuous R.T. Chatter between air traffic controllers and pilots speaking English in the various accents of the world that it probably all began at Ely on that bleak afternoon of 23 September 1911.

Hucks continued his demonstrations on Monday, Tuesday and Wednesday of the following week, accepting an invitation to lunch hosted by prominent local businessmen at the Exchange Club on Tuesday. He left Ely at 6.16 a.m. on Thursday 28 September for his next venue at Shaftesbury Park, Newport, indulging for fun in an unofficial race with some friends in a motor car. They were given a ten-minute start and, although Hucks completed the journey in twenty-one minutes, they arrived two minutes ahead of him.

The tour continued to Gloucester and terminated at Cheltenham on 21 October, Hucks having completed an estimated 1,000 miles of flying in ninety separate flights.

Despite abysmal weather, aviation advanced apace through 1912. In January the formation of the Cardiff Aero Club was announced with headquarters at 114 Miskin Street, the business address of its secretary. The club's activities, which were regularly reported in *Flight* and the local press were mainly confined to the building and flying of models and kites, although a full-sized glider was stated to be under construction when all reports of the club's activities ceased in July 1912.

Ernest Sutton suffered a severe setback on 4 March when his hangar collapsed during a great gale that raged across the land, totally wrecking the Blériot inside. Worse troubles lay in store for him, however. The Sutton Bros motor business was already in dire financial straits when, in response to an advertisement, he travelled to Paris to offer his services as an aviator to the Turkish Government, whose armed forces were engaged in a bitter struggle with an Italian expeditionary force that had invaded the Turkish possession of Tripoli, now Libya. His journey was in vain and he returned to Swansea to face the music. In May he was adjudged bankrupt in a hearing in which it was stated that his brother, also bankrupt, had fled the country.

The resilient Sutton then set himself up in business as a consulting engineer with premises at 37 Worcester Place, Swansea. He was presumably reasonably successful for he was able to afford a course of flying lessons at the W.H. Ewan flying school at the London Aerodrome, Hendon, that culminated in the grant of Royal Aero Club Aviator's Certificate, No.295, in September 1912.

In May 1912, newspaper magnate and aviation enthusiast Lord Northcliffe inaugurated 'The Daily Mail Aeroplane Scheme', its object being to publicise aviation by sending forth well known aviators on tours of the United Kingdom. The first aviator to participate, and the one who visited South Wales, was Frenchman Henri Salmet.

Born in Paris in 1878, Salmet had enjoyed a meteoric rise to fame since arriving in England to work as a mechanic at the Blériot School of Flying at Hendon. Having learned to fly and gained Aviator's Certificate No.99 in 1911, he had by October of that year been appointed chief instructor of the school, a position that did not preclude finding the time to indulge in a number of record attempts. As a result he had raised the United Kingdom altitude record to 8,070ft in November 1911 and was the current holder of the London–Paris speed record following a flight from Hendon to Issy-les-Moulineaux in three hours sixteen minutes. Throughout the tour he piloted a 50hp Gnome-powered Blériot of distinctive appearance due to the fact that the normally exposed rear fuselage framework had been covered with fabric as an aid to flotation in the event of ditching.

Salmet's tour commenced at Wormwood Scrubs on Thursday 16 May and progressed via Taplow, Reading, Marlborough and Bath to Mangotsfield, near Bristol, where he arrived on 18 May. Inclement weather impeded further progress until 22 May when he landed in a farmer's field off Bassaleg Road, Newport, bearing the first air freight to cross the Bristol Channel – a sack of potatoes donated by the market gardener who had housed the machine at Mangotsfield to a friend, Mr J. Flood of Pontypool. Later he continued flying in cold, showery and gusty conditions to the Sophia Gardens, Cardiff, from where he made a number of exhibition flights the following day.

Weather conditions were no better on Friday 26 May when Salmet left Cardiff bound for Swansea. Crowds assembled at vantage points along the coast to watch the aviator pass by and such was the excitement in Swansea itself that work came to a virtual standstill. Roofs were packed with spectators and an enormous crowd assembled on the sands where Salmet was expected to land at 4.30 p.m. However, the appointed time came and went and the aeroplane failed to appear. It later transpired that, on approaching Briton Ferry, Salmet had encountered a shower of such severity that he had deemed it prudent to discontinue the flight and, to that end, had landed on a large expanse of flat green land nearby. The Blériot stopped with startling suddenness. He had landed in the Crymlyn Bog!

Happily no damage was done and with the aid of several factory workers, three constables and a local journalist, Salmet was able to extricate the aeroplane from the mire and, when conditions improved, continue his journey to Swansea where he circled the sands before landing. There ensued a rush of spectators towards the aeroplane that the police found impossible to restrain and which threatened to damage the frail machine. 'Don't push', shouted an alarmed Salmet in his somewhat quaint English, 'If I see one push I will put my hand on his nose.' When order was restored he gave an exhibition flight before proceeding to a civic reception and an appearance on the stage of the Swansea Empire from where he gave a short address to the enthralled audience.

The following afternoon an estimated 25,000 local citizens assembled on the sands to take their leave of the aviator when he departed on the next leg of his journey to Llanelli Cricket Ground where stumps were drawn early to enable him to land to another enthusiastic reception. He remained at Llanelli until 29 May when he departed for Weston-super-Mare. Having wisely elected to take the short water crossing still used by prudent pilots of single-engined aeroplanes to this day, he retraced his route to Lavernock near Penarth. It is difficult to appreciate today the excitement that such a flight was capable of producing. Contemporary reports describe Llanelli hospital patients being wheeled out to watch, Swansea Sands and the hills above Port Talbot being black with people and large crowds assembling on the seafronts at Porthcawl and Barry just to watch the aviator fly by.

Salmet spent the following month demonstrating the Blériot in the West Country, returning to the Sophia Gardens on 26 June. It was his intention to continue to Pontypridd the following day but inclement weather and mechanical problems en route compelled him to return to the Sophia Gardens. Sickness then intervened and Salmet returned to London for treatment leaving the aeroplane at Sophia Gardens. He returned on 18 July and, after giving a final exhibition at the Cardiff Horticultural Society Show, then in progress at the gardens, their first involvement with aircraft of any sort since Stanley Spencer's fiasco eighteen years previously, departed for Ross on Wye where he arrived a day late having made a forced landing at Raglan en route.

An intriguing lot among the inventory of assets of the Atlas Engineering Works, Canton, Cardiff, sold by public auction on 12 August 1912 was described as 'a 35-40 horse-power Madaler monoplane, to carry a pilot and one passenger. The machine is guaranteed to develop any speed up to 70 miles an hour.' An accompanying photograph depicts a high wing monoplane somewhat reminiscent of a Santos-Dumont 'Demoiselle'. Bidding commenced at £1, the machine being knocked down for £10 to a representative of Messrs Harris & Co. Ltd, motor engineers of Abergavenny. Its subsequent history does not appear to have been recorded.

A flying display was the principal attraction of the Glamorgan National Reserve Military Tournament held at Virginia Park, Caerphilly, on 31 August 1912, one of the few fine days of that miserable summer. The aviator, H.J.D. Astley, a twenty-four-year-old Old Etonian, was a well-known figure in motor racing and aviation circles as well as in London society where he was reputedly one of the best-dressed men in the West End. The holder of Aviator's Certificate No.48 he piloted a Blériot XI. There is sometimes confusion over this point as the machine is sometimes referred to as a Birdling Monoplane, the name bestowed on Blériot XIs built under licence in the United Kingdom by the Universal Aviation Co.

A crowd reported to be 20,000 strong witnessed an exciting programme of events that resulted in several participants being removed senseless from the arena before it was Astley's turn to perform. He took off at 5.00 p.m. amid tumultuous applause and set off on a wide circular sweep in the direction of Bedwas and Machen. He did not reappear. Ignition problems necessitated a forced landing at Tylaglyn Farm, near Bedwas, and although the machine was undamaged the fault could not be rectified and it remained at the farm until removed by road the following day. The tournament organisers obviously felt that they had not received value for their money for on 5 December 1912 The Royal Aero Club Arbitration Committee heard the case of Aeros Ltd, Astley's agents *v*. The Committee of the Glamorgan National Reserve Military Tournament when Aeros Ltd claimed the balance of £60 owing for the display. They were awarded £40. Astley was not present to hear the judgement for he had been killed in an accident at a similar display at the Balmoral Showground, Belfast, on 12 September 1912, just twelve days after his Caerphilly performance.

The final opportunity for local aeroplane spotters that year occurred on 20 September when that truly intrepid aviator Denys Corbett-Wilson crossed the county en route from Paris to his home at Kilkenny in southern Ireland. Corbett-Wilson had made history on 17 April 1912 when he had flown from Fishguard to Enniscorthy, becoming the first aviator to cross the Irish Sea in the process. On the flight in question he had flown in stages from Paris to Caerwent and was on the next leg of his journey to Goodwick, near Fishguard. The following day he crossed the Irish Sea for the second time in his career landing at Gorey, County Wexford, due to bad weather before continuing his journey to Kilkenny.

The people of Barry and Penarth had the unexpected opportunity to view an aeroplane at close quarters on 5 May 1913 when the British-built Blériot monoplane of the well-known demonstration pilot Sydney Pickles was forced to land at both places. Pickles, a cheerful twenty-two-year-old cigarette-smoking Australian, the holder of Aviator's certificate No.263, had made a series of demonstration flights from Stradey Park, Llanelli, between 1 and 3 May in the course of which he had attained an altitude of 9,000ft above Gower and carried South Wales' first aeroplane passenger, Mr Rees Jenkins of Tyla Morris, Briton Ferry. Having spent Sunday at Llanelli, he departed on Monday morning intending to fly to Winchester. He routed along to the South Wales coast, intending to make the short water crossing from Lavernock to Weston-super-Mare, but on approaching Barry his 80hp Anzani engine began to lose oil pressure due to that most common of causes, loss of oil. He elected to make a precautionary landing to remedy the situation and brought the monoplane low over Romilly Park to a gentle touchdown in a meadow belonging to Cold Knap Farm, an area now covered by housing immediately to the east of the present marine lake, at about 1.30 p.m.

Having purchased some oil from a local garage he took off to resume his journey, barely clearing the pebble bank at Cold Knap beach. After circling the area at low level, he continued towards Lavernock where he turned towards Weston. However, he found conditions over the Channel so hazy that he experienced difficulty in maintaining control of the aeroplane.

Edwin Prosser with his Caudron biplane at Ely racecourse, Cardiff, 20 September 1913. (Mr & Mrs A.R. German)

It is surprisingly difficult in hazy conditions to differentiate between the surface of a calm sea and the sky and, without sight of the natural horizon or the benefit of blind flying instruments that had not been developed at that time, a pilot can easily become disorientated and lose control of his aeroplane. Pickles returned to Lavernock only to discover that his engine was losing oil again and another precautionary landing ensued. He made his approach over Redlands Road, just clearing the rooftops, and landed in a field belonging to Cornerswell Farm where the Blériot was housed in a barn prior to continuing its journey by train.

Pickles' recalcitrant engine was to let him down badly again a few weeks later during a display at Dundee. In the course of the ensuing forced landing the Blériot struck the chimney of a house, crashed 30ft to the ground and was wrecked, Pickles being fortunate to escape without injury.

An unidentified aeroplane reported to have flown over Cardiff on 8 August 1913 was almost certainly the Morane Saulnier monoplane of Gustav Hamel who gave a flying demonstration at Llanwrtyd Wells a few days later and who was to give a sensational display at Cardiff the following year.

It was a race, run as the result of a wager, between Hamel and his friend B.C. Hucks over a course starting and finishing at Birmingham on 30 August 1913 that inspired Edwin Prosser, a young Birmingham aviator who witnessed it, to issue a similar challenge to his friend and fellow aviator M.F. Glew, who readily accepted – the stakes being £100. Both Glew and Prosser were eighteen-year-old recently qualified aviators holding certificates Nos 410 and 526 respectively, the numbers being indicative of the rapid proliferation of active aviators at that time.

Above and below: *M.F. Glew and his Blackburn monoplane in 1913. This aeroplane is now in the possession of the Shuttleworth Trust at Old Warden, Bedfordshire, and is (at the time of writing) the oldest airworthy British aeroplane.* (P.H.T. Green collection)

As Prosser, an itinerant demonstration pilot, was due to fly at Ely Racecourse, Cardiff, it was agreed that the race would start and finish there on the afternoon of Saturday 13 September 1913. As in the case of the Birmingham contest, it was to be run in stages with intermediate landings at Island Farm, Bridgend, Cimla Park, Neath and Clyne Valley Racecourse, Swansea, before the final dash back to Ely.

Race day dawned overcast and windy. Glew, together with his aeroplane, a 50hp Gnome powered Blackburn type D monoplane, arrived at Ely in the morning having travelled from his Northamptonshire home by train. Prosser's journey to Cardiff was somewhat more eventful. Some days previously while giving an exhibition flight at Abergavenny the 45hp Anzani engine of his Caudron biplane had suffered a dropped valve and as a result he had remained grounded awaiting repairs until early on Saturday afternoon.

He eventually departed Abergavenny at 1.23 p.m., carrying a load of specially wrapped copies of the *South Wales Evening Express* to be dropped en route, the lucky finders, of whom there were fifteen, were to be rewarded by a 1s prize.

At 2.50 p.m. spectators at Ely who were equipped with telescopes reported sighting the Caudron appearing from the east and some eight minutes later Prosser, piloting the only biplane to fly in the county prior to the First World War, touched down on Ely's turf. He had quite a tale to tell.

He had flown for most of the journey at an altitude of 3,500ft into the teeth of a headwind so strong that on occasions he had found himself to be travelling backwards. Having encountered two heavy showers that soaked him to the skin, he had been compelled to spend some fifteen minutes on the ground in the vicinity of Newport in order to restore the feeling in his hands. When he finally arrived at Ely his fuel supply was almost exhausted and the Caudron was found to have suffered minor airframe damage due to the buffeting it had received.

While Prosser's machine was undergoing repairs Glew made two attempts to fly in order to keep the crowd amused, but only succeeded in wrenching a tyre from the wheel rim on one occasion and bending the axle of his undercarriage on the other. Engine problems with Prosser's machine further delayed the proceedings before the weather played its final card and the race was abandoned in the face of gale force winds and torrential driving rain. The bedraggled and disappointed spectators at Ely and the staging points had their money refunded and Glew and the Blackburn returned to Northampton by train.

Prosser, however, remained in the district for some time. On 15 September he flew twice from Ely rising high above the Bristol Channel on both occasions. The second flight terminated due to engine trouble at Cogan Hall Farm, Lower Penarth, where a search party from Ely discovered the aviator signing the autograph books of numerous admiring young ladies. The Caudron and its pilot were eventually returned to Ely by road.

On 20 September Prosser made a successful series of demonstration flights from Ely, in the course of which he climbed to an enormous height above the field and also caused a sensation by flying so low along the railway line that he passed between the chimney stacks of the Ely Brewery and Crosswells Brewery that stood on either side of it immediately to the north of Cowbridge Road.

Prosser's itinerary then took him in a westerly direction. On 29 September he landed, whether by accident or design is not recorded, at Mount Pleasant Farm, Cowbridge. It was a fair day and an auction of rams that was in progress at the time came to an abrupt end as the bidders stampeded from the ring to view the aeroplane. One disconsolate farmer was quoted as remarking to a *Glamorgan Gazette* representative: 'Bother that old flying man, if that blooming thing hadn't come all my rams would have been sold.'

Precise details of Prosser's movements after that have proved impossible to uncover. On Sunday 4 October an exhibition from a field off Ewenny Road, Bridgend, was described almost lyrically by the *Glamorgan Gazette* as 'the prettiest, smartest and most wonderful flying exhibition yet seen in these parts.' The writer went on to say, 'Perhaps no-one who was there had ever seen better and the minds of all were full of wonder and amazement.'

The following Monday he moved on to Margam where, in the vicinity of Margam Mountain, he encountered turbulence of such severity that he was almost thrown out of the aeroplane. He gave a display at Margam that evening; the venue is not recorded. He arrived at Neath, probably Cimla Park, on 9 October and gave an exhibition there on 13 October. Further exhibitions are recorded at Seven Sisters on an unspecified date and the Athletic Ground, Pontardawe, on the 23rd. Other exhibitions outside the county took place at Ammanford, Llanwrtyd Wells and Brecon. It was during an attempted flight from Brecon to an intended display at Aberdare on 1 November that the Caudron was caught by a severe gust of wind on take off, sideslipped into the ground and received damage of sufficient severity to cause the cancellation of the remainder of Prosser's proposed itinerary.

On 27 August 1913 Lt Nesterov of the Imperial Russian Army who was piloting a Nieuport Type IV monoplane near Kiev found something new to do with an aeroplane. Having dived to gain airspeed he pulled up into an ever steepening climb until the Nieuport's flightpath passed through the vertical and the inverted, then back into a dive from which it recovered to level flight at its starting point, having described a vertical circle in the air. The art of aerobatics had been born. Soon afterwards the French aviator Adolphe Pegoud, flying a specially strengthened Blériot monoplane with larger, more powerful elevators and a fuel system capable of functioning when the aeroplane was inverted, began to perform similar manoeuvres and on 21 September advanced a stage further when he discontinued the vertical circle half way around and flew off inverted. The first Englishman to join the ranks of the aerobatic pilots was B.C. Hucks who acquired a Blériot similar to Pegoud's machine and first described a vertical circle in November 1913.

Aerobatic flight added a new dimension to display flying and has remained a popular public entertainment ever since. The vertical circle manoeuvre was soon christened 'looping the loop' after a circus bicycle act, popular at the time, in which the cyclist pedalled furiously around a vertical loop shaped track and, provided sufficient speed was maintained, was able to keep himself in the saddle and the bicycle on the track due to the influence of centripetal force. Today the manoeuvre is known simply as a loop.

Exhibitions of looping the loop soon became all the rage and the population of Cardiff did not have long to wait to witness the latest wonder of the aviation world, only until March 1914 in fact when Gustav Hamel visited Ely Racecourse and gave a series of memorable exhibition flights.

Tall, blonde and handsome, twenty-four-year-old Hamel was, despite his Germanic sounding name, a British subject. The son of an eminent London surgeon he had learned to fly at the Blériot School at Pau and was awarded a French aviator's certificate on 6 February 1911. On his return to the United Kingdom, he qualified for a Royal Aero Club certificate,

Gustav Hamel with his Morane-Saulnier monoplane at Ely racecourse, Cardiff, 28 March 1914. (Mr & Mrs A.R. German)

No.64, a few days later. His subsequent activities as a demonstration and racing pilot had made him a household name throughout the land and it was only to be expected that he would add aerobatic flying to his repertoire.

Hamel's first Cardiff demonstration at the controls of his Morane-Saulnier monoplane, the upper wing surfaces of which were decorated with roundels in order to make it evident to spectators when the aeroplane was inverted, took place on 25 March before a disappointingly small crowd due to inclement weather conditions that obliged him to postpone his take off until 4.30 p.m.

Once airborne he climbed to about 1,000ft and performed several loops before flying over the city. He returned to Ely and looped once more before concluding the display with a spectacular high speed, low level flypast that left a party of officials, over whom he had passed at a height of about 2ft, prostrate on the grass and a public address telephone cable that he had failed to notice, severed.

The following day he flew to Caerleon Racecourse where he gave a similar demonstration and on the return journey demonstrated the determined spirit that was ultimately to prove his undoing. Despite a violent thunderstorm that had developed over the Cardiff area, Hamel and his passenger Baron Gunsberg took off as planned. Flying at a height of 600ft in order to maintain visual contact with the ground they were buffeted by severe turbulence, lashed by torrential rain and half blinded by lightning flashes, the attendant thunder being clearly audible above the noise of the engine. They landed safely from that foolhardy escapade after a flight of fifteen minutes.

Gustav Hamel looping his Morane-Saulmier monoplane over Ely racecourse, Cardiff, 28 March 1914.
(Mr & Mrs A.R. German)

Hamel was airborne again on Friday when he made a short flight over the docks 'in order to amuse himself' carrying as a passenger local flying enthusiast Signore Arioli.

The highlight of his week at Cardiff came on Saturday 28 March when he flew from Ely before a crowd of some 8,000 people that included among its number the Marchioness of Bute and her family and the Lord Mayor. 'The occasion bringing together one of the finest collections of cars ever seen in South Wales (from Rolls-Royce to Ford)... The social world of South Wales collected in force and all the best known faces were evidently out for the afternoon', reported *The Western Mail*.

The entertainment began with an exhibition of looping over Ely followed by a flight in the course of which Hamel flew over the city 'looping continuously'. It concluded with a series of seven passenger flights, carrying among others Mr C.H. Watkins (see next chapter) who 'conducted a series of experiments in standing and moving about in the air.'

Another flight, reserved for the holder of the winning admission ticket, presented the organisers with some difficulty. The first winner failed to make himself known and the second, a young married man, was prevented by his father from boarding the aeroplane. He therefore reluctantly sold the ticket for three pounds and donated the proceeds to charity. The purchaser Capt. Mikkelson, the Norwegian master of the SS *Stronsia*, berthed at Barry, who obviously came from adventurous stock – his brother Agnar Mikkelson, an explorer, had recently reappeared having been lost with a companion in Greenland for two years – so enjoyed the experience that he donated a further 10s to the funds of Cardiff Royal Infirmary.

Less than two months later, on 23 May 1914, Hamel left Villacoublay, Paris, in appalling weather conditions bound for Hendon where he was due to compete in the London Aerial Derby. He failed to arrive at his destination and no trace of him or his aeroplane was ever discovered.

Spectacular though Hamel's displays may have been they were undoubtedly eclipsed by those given by B.C. Hucks at the Sophia Gardens, Cardiff, in June 1914. Hucks, who had become a freelance aviator and switched allegiance from Blackburn to Blériot in 1912, had, like Hamel, become a household name as a result of his years of display flying throughout the length and breadth of the land.

His aeroplanes, an 80hp Gnome-powered two-seater and a 50hp Gnome-powered 'looper', complete with inverted fuel system in which he had executed 550 loops since the previous autumn, arrived in Cardiff by surface transport and, from 16 June were exhibited at Messrs James Howells and Co.'s garage at Wharton Street, awaiting the arrival of their pilot who, once more the possessor of a driving licence, arrived by motor car on 18 June and installed himself in the Royal Hotel. Having been entertained to lunch at the Exchange Club, Hucks made a short flight over the city in the afternoon to publicise his forthcoming performances, after which he described operating from the Sophia Gardens as like flying out of a cup. His first exhibition took place that evening. Cardiff had never seen the like and is unlikely to see the like again. Nowadays any pilot attempting such feats would probably receive a custodial sentence allowing time to reflect on the formidable list of offences relating to low flying and flight over built-up areas committed.

After two flights in the two-seater during which he circled the City Hall at near rooftop level, Hucks boarded the looper and gave the 4,000 spectators the exhibition they had paid to witness, a fourteen-minute aerobatic flight. Having made a number of steep turns over the gardens he flew towards the Civic Centre where he executed five loops in quick succession before returning to the gardens and executing a further three above the heads of the spectators. He then made for Llandaff where he inverted the Blériot prior to making an inverted fly past over the city, regaining level flight when above the castle. Hucks had prepared himself for his inverted flights by tying himself to a kitchen chair and being held upside down by friends for increasingly lengthy periods of time. What his neighbours must have thought defies imagination. After several more loops he landed to a reception reminiscent of Salmet's arrival at Swansea. The police lost all control of the crowd and further flying, which was to have included a number of passenger flights, had to be abandoned.

A similar performance on Friday included a height-guessing competition for a prize of £5 and three passenger flights. One passenger being the Chief Constable, Mr David Williams, who Hucks, doubtless still mindful of his discomfiture at the hands of the Cardiff City Police five years previously, jokingly offered to drop off over the law courts. Two performances ensued on Saturday. During the afternoon two passenger flights, one to Caerphilly and one to Penarth regatta, were carried out and the first ciné film of Cardiff from aloft was shot. Hucks had extended an invitation to his old next-door neighbour Mr Frederick Hall Thomas, better known as Fred Welsh, the Cardiff pugilist who was destined to become lightweight champion of the world on 7 July, to accompany him that afternoon but Mr Thomas was 'unavoidably detained' in London.

The finale on Saturday evening included an exhibition of 'steeple chasing' in which Hucks flew the two-seater at very low level above the bed of the River Taff from Llandaff, 'jumped' over the old Cardiff Bridge that carried Cowbridge Road, and flew past the front door of his old house, 8 Coldstream Terrace, prior to 'jumping' Wood Street Bridge. On landing it was discovered that, like Hamel at Ely, he had encountered an unseen telephone wire that had inflicted some damage to his propeller and, although he flew several more times that evening he declined to carry a number of booked passengers for reasons of safety.

The following month the assassination of the Archduke Franz Ferdinand at Sarajevo had precipitated a chain of events outside the scope of this history that with startling suddenness brought about the first punctuation mark of the twentieth century, the First World War.

8

The Enigma of the Watkins Monoplane

It is impossible to discuss early aviation in South Wales without making reference to the Watkins Monoplane currently on display in the foyer of the National Museums & Galleries of Wales, Cardiff. Superficially similar to the Blériot line of monoplanes, it was donated by its designer/builder Mr C.H. Watkins to the Historic Aircraft Collection at RAF St Athan in 1962 following many years in storage at his home in Colum Road, Cardiff. Later it was passed to the National Museum.

Horace Watkins was born in Cardiff in 1887, trained in motor engineering and undoubtedly developed into a skilled and innovative engineer. In later years he also appears to have developed into a skilled and innovative storyteller.

According to Mr Watkins, who was wont to tell the story to anyone willing to listen, design work on the aeroplane commenced in 1907. In 1908 he took out a lease on a shed at Llys, Tal-y-Bont Farm, Maindy, Cardiff, where the machine was constructed. Referred to variously as the C.H.W. Mono or the Robin Goch, the first flight took place in 1909 and by 1910 flights had been made to Caerphilly and the top of the Garth Mountain. Later he commenced night flying using two plumb bobs of 10 and 20ft length which activated lights in the cockpit to assist in gauging height during landing. Flying activities ceased with the outbreak of hostilities in 1914 and the aeroplane did not fly again.

Following four years war work in the aircraft industry Watkins returned to Cardiff where he spent the remainder of his working life as a consulting engineer. His story has been accepted without question by many people for many years but is it credible? In order to attempt to determine the truth it is necessary to examine such evidence as exists.

There is certainly some photographic evidence that Watkins was involved in aeroplane construction, almost certainly before 1914. One photograph, probably the earliest, depicts him seated in an engineless uncovered fuselage supported by an undercarriage structure incorporating a long skid which held the rear of the fuselage clear of the ground. The (apparently) warping wings, although supported by upper and lower bracing wires, appear to have been so insecurely attached to the fuselage that they would probably have separated from it had the aeroplane ever become airborne. Two other photographs show an aeroplane with an engine installed. In one the wingless fuselage is supported by a metal reverse tricycle undercarriage while in the other, a head on view, some sort of tail skid arrangement is apparent. No photographs of a complete aeroplane with its engine running or airborne appear to exist, which must cast doubts over Watkins' claims.

Much the same can be said of documentary evidence. In common with other amateur aircraft constructors of the day, most of whom never flew, Horace Watkins' activities did warrant a certain amount of newspaper coverage but only from late 1913 onwards. The *South Wales Daily News* of 13 September 1913, when commenting on a proposed aviation meeting in the Sophia Gardens, Cardiff, mentioned proposed 'trials of a new type of flying craft built locally by Mr Watkins of Colum Rd.' The meeting, however, did not take place.

Above and opposite: *The Watkins monoplane in its various guises prior to the First World War. No dates given for these photographs can be considered reliable. Note the warping wings.* (National Museums & Galleries of Wales)

The *Western Mail* of 7 January 1914 carried a lengthy article on Watkins and his aeroplane stating that '...after three years hard work he has completed an aeroplane which in some important features is believed to excel any machine, yet built.' The article went on to detail Watkins' claims for the aeroplane. He claimed 40hp for his beautifully home-made engine, a weight of 3cwt (presumably unladen), a take-off run of 30 yards and a maximum speed of 70mph. Watkins was also stated to be working on another model and one of the latter paragraphs contained the sentence 'Mr Watkins may be expected to be seen flying around Cardiff a great deal in the future.' There was, however, no suggestion that the aeroplane had actually flown at the time of writing. The final mention of Watkins prior to the First World War appeared in the *Western Mail* of 30 March 1914 when, reporting his flight with Gustav Hamel, the paper described him as 'a young Cardiff aviator.'

However, it is the lack of newspaper reports of any flights by Watkins that casts further doubts upon his claims. Every flight made by E.T. Willows was reported in depth, as were all flights to, from and over Cardiff prior to 1914. The *Western Mail* of 2 September 1911 somewhat tantalisingly described B.C. Hucks as '...the first aviator, so far as is known, to circle Cardiff with a monoplane', which suggests that that very air-minded journal had no knowledge of any activities by Watkins at that time. Certainly Watkins was no shrinking violet where publicity was concerned and there is no doubt that he would have taken steps to publicise any successful flights, besides which it is virtually impossible to keep the flight of any aircraft secret. Bearing in mind that the first tentative flights in Great Britain took place in 1908, a flight in 1910 from Maindy to Caerphilly would have been a sensational feat witnessed by thousands and widely reported. Even in 1914 such a flight by a local man would have been worthy of considerable comment.

Further mystery surrounds the aeroplane now on display inasmuch as it hardly resembles the aeroplane or aeroplanes depicted in the early photographs. The single camber warping

C.H. Watkins (left) with Gustav Hamel (centre) and Hamel's secretary in March 1914 at Cardiff. (National Museums & Galleries of Wales)

The Watkins monoplane as it is today. Note the wings now have ailerons. (National Museums & Galleries of Wales)

wings have been replaced by relatively thick double camber wings fitted with ailerons, considerably later technology. The tailplane has been raised to the top of the fuselage and the undercarriage, incorporating a sprung skid just aft of the cockpit, also differs considerably from any in the photographs. Finally, the empty weight of 680lb is just over twice the 336lb claimed by Watkins in 1914 probably at least in part due to the new wings. When the above modifications were carried out is impossible to determine but photographic evidence suggests that the machine was in its present configuration when it was exhibited at the Welsh Industries Fair in 1938.

The final unanswered question is: 'Is the aeroplane capable of flight?' Short of somebody attempting to fly it that question will never be answered for certain but in the opinion of people more expert in the field of aeronautical engineering than myself the answer is probably no. The essentially similar Blériot XI aeroplane with an empty weight of 484lb was not a spritely performer. With an empty weight some forty per cent greater and a similar power unit it is doubtful if the Watkins monoplane as currently configured is capable of leaving the ground.

In summary, there can be little doubt that Horace Watkins was involved in aeroplane construction prior to the First World War. However, we only have Watkins' word that the aeroplane ever flew. Whether he ever taxied, hopped, skipped or carried out the more ambitious feats that he claimed is a secret that he took to his grave in 1976. However, the lack of any photographic documentary and eyewitness evidence of any such flights must cast serious doubts on Watkins' claims.

9
The First World War

The First World War was the first conflict in history in which aircraft played a significant role. Just how significant can be judged by considering the fact that in just four years Britain's aerial strength grew from some 150 machines to about 22,000, most of them of previously unimagined performance and size. Yet, by a happy accident of geography, that first great air war passed south east Wales by.

The reasons are quire easy to see. With the exception of flying training, none of which was carried out in Wales, the majority of aerial action took place overseas. The only operational flying at home by Britain's two air arms, The Royal Flying Corps, a branch of the Army, and the Royal Naval Air Service, was in defence of the realm against air attack and the protection of shipping around our shores from the very serious threat imposed by German U-boats.

South Wales was judged not to be in any great danger from attack by the Zeppelin and Schütte Lanz rigid airships, which mounted fifty-three raids on England and Scotland between 1915 and 1917, and was well beyond the range of the Gotha IV and Staaken bombers, which caused considerable damage and casualties in south east England in 1917. Consequently the only concession to air defence was the introduction of interim lighting restrictions, which empowered the authorities to impose a blackout, covering Monmouthshire, Cardiff, Penarth and Barry, effective from 14 April 1916. In the event they never needed to be implemented.

On the other hand, the county was too far to the east to play a part in the war against the U-boats, a grim struggle that nearly brought the country to its knees. It is true to say that the U-boat blockade which commenced on 4 February 1915 struck closer to home than any air attacks. For instance, the SS *Bengrove*, a collier of 2,398 tons, outward bound from Barry, was torpedoed and sunk by the U-20 when five miles N.N.E. of Ilfracombe on 7 March 1915, happily without loss of life. Several more vessels followed her to the bottom in the Lundy area in the ensuing weeks.

However, the countermeasures against U-boat incursions were deployed further to the west. They consisted of standing patrols mounted by surface vessels supported by airships of the SS, Coastal and SSZ classes operating from Mullion, Bude and Pembroke, seaplanes based at Newlyn and Fishguard and aeroplanes based at Salcombe, Mullion and Pembroke. The result of that activity was to deny the U-boats access to the Bristol Channel east of a line running roughly north to south through Lundy.

As a consequence of the preceding, no aircraft were ever based in the county and very few were seen. There is some anecdotal evidence, which cannot be substantiated, that airships sometimes operated as far east as Barry and Cardiff and certainly one, the *SSZ37*, was damaged in a forced landing near Mumbles Head. However, the level of aerial activity can best be judged by the fact that throughout the war the editor of the *Barry Dock News* felt that the passage of an aeroplane over the district was an event worthy of mention.

Workers at the Willows Balloon factory, Westgate Street, Cardiff, c.1918. (National Museums & Galleries of Wales)

Despite the lack of visible aerial activity during the conflict, several South Wales firms did play a supporting role. As can be imagined the enormous increase in Britain's air power was not achieved without an associated enormous increase in aircraft production. Despite major expansion the small number of British aircraft manufacturers were unable to cope with the demand and were joined by many other companies mostly drawn from the joinery trade who built either components or in some cases entire aircraft. Several such companies, Boulton Paul for example, later became major aircraft manufacturers in their own right.

Two local companies are worthy of mention – Cambrian Aircraft Constructors and the Willows Aircraft Co. Cambrian Aircraft Constructors was formed in 1917 by three prominent members of the timber trade, Messrs T.W. David, T.L. Demery and D. Morgan Rees. From small beginnings in a woodshed in Tyndal Street, East Moors, Cardiff, the company later occupied a large warehouse nearby and in February 1918 opened a second facility at 18 Station Road, Penarth. The company built wings, ailerons and undercarriage components for D.H.10 aircraft using silver spruce imported from British Columbia. Little of that very expensive wood was wasted, the off-cuts being used for the manufacture of children's toys, which were in short supply at the time. At its peak the workforce, consisting largely of women who had been trained at Cardiff Technical College, exceeded 500. However, with the coming of peace the requirement for new aircraft diminished sharply and after unsuccessful attempts to diversify into other joinery work the company ceased operations in September 1919.

One of the countermeasures adopted against bombing attacks on south east England was the balloon barrage. The barrages, which totalled ten in number by the end of the war, consisted of a series of tethered balloons, joined by horizontal cables from which dangled further cables which collectively formed what was known as an apron. Flown at altitudes of up to 10,000ft the balloons and their attendant aprons compelled the bombers to attack from high level thereby reducing the accuracy of their aim.

Over 100 balloons were required to maintain the barrages and contracts were placed with various manufacturers as a matter of urgency. One such manufacturer was the hitherto dormant Willows Aircraft Co. Having been released from his military service which, as has already been mentioned, involved work on balloons, Ernest Willows returned to Cardiff early in 1918 and established a manufacturing facility in the American Roller Skating Rink in Westgate Street. There his predominantly female staff produced a significant number of balloons until the cessation of hostilities. As in the case of Cambrian Aircraft Constructors, demand dried up with the advent of peace and the factory closed in 1919.

In November 1918 the 'war to end all wars' came to an end and the weary people of the world looked forward to an era of everlasting peace. How wrong they were!

10
The Year 1919

The year 1919, the first year of peace, appears to have been unlike any other year in British history. Four million demobilised servicemen returned home, many permanently scarred in body and mind by their experiences, but nevertheless more fortunate than the 750,000 members of the armed forces and Mercantile Marine who were destined never to return. Many displayed an air of conscious pride in their service, exemplified, for instance, by the retention of naval and military titles that was a feature of British life for decades to follow, the reverse side of the coin being the contempt in which those who had not served, for whatever reason, were frequently held. Newspapers published letters, penned in bellicose fashion, calling for the execution of the Kaiser and retribution against the German people alongside pathetic small advertisements from grieving relatives appealing for information as to the fate of missing loved ones most of whom had either been blown to pieces or ground into the soil of France. Some expected life to continue as before but it soon became apparent that the old order was crumbling and that the long slow march towards a more egalitarian society had begun.

Four years of war had changed aviation beyond recognition. Vast quantities of aeroplanes had been produced and thousands of young men had been trained to fly them. At the cessation of hostilities the majority of both were declared surplus to requirements and a small number of redundant men and machines formed the nucleus of an emergent civil aviation industry.

Civil aviation was generally permitted from 1 May although restrictions were briefly lifted during the Easter holidays to permit a limited amount of joy riding, mostly in the London area. Throughout the land, numerous air transport undertakings were proposed but few progressed beyond the pipe dreams of their proposers. For instance, in Cardiff the directors of Cambrian Aircraft Constructors Ltd, registered Cambrian Aerial Travel Ltd, whose stated objectives were: 'To maintain aircraft lines and services, etc.', but nothing came of the proposed venture. The majority of air transport operators who did materialise were either subsidiary companies of the major aircraft manufacturers or concerns operating a few small aeroplanes, purchased at knock-down prices, who engaged largely in joy riding. The immediate post-war years were a time of relative economic prosperity and a time when the British people exhibited a determination to enjoy themselves to the full after the dark days of war. Aviation was still a novelty, aeroplanes and fuel were cheap and an apparently inexhaustible supply of passengers willing to pay a guinea per head to fly two at a time on five minute flights must have convinced such operators that they had found their own private El Dorado. Over fifty such concerns sprang up immediately after the war but the majority folded with the deteriorating economic situation that prevailed from 1921 onwards.

The first post-war civil aeroplane to grace the skies of Glamorgan was probably a Handley Page H.P.12, a rudimentary civil conversion of the giant H.P. 0/400 biplane bomber powered by two 360hp Rolls-Royce Eagle VIII engines. Operated by a subsidiary company of its manufacturers, Handley Page Transport Ltd, on charter to the *Daily Mail*, it left its base at Cricklewood at 6.00 a.m. on 9 May under the command of Lt H.M.D. Walker with copies of that newspaper loaded into cells that had replaced the original bomb bays. The newspapers were dropped by Guardian Angel parachute at an unspecified site at Cardiff and into Victoria Park, Swansea, after which the aeroplane set course for Filton Aerodrome near Bristol where it landed at 9.00 a.m. The flight was merely a publicity stunt, there being no serious intention of using such an uneconomic method of newspaper distribution on a regular basis.

Shortly afterwards, on 17 May the first joy riding operation commenced when Capt. E.D.C. Herne, the son of a former Cardiff solicitor, began carrying passengers from Lock's Common at the popular seaside resort of Porthcawl. Herne owned two Armstrong Whitworth F.K.3 aeroplanes powered by RAF1A engines, registered G-EABY and G-EABZ and named *Porthcawl* and *Rhondda* respectively. In common with many operators in that very early post-war period it appears that Herne did not bother to apply the civil registration letters, the machines retaining instead their original military serials of B9629 and B9518. Whether he flew both aeroplanes at Porthcawl is unclear, certainly G-EABY *Porthcawl* was used. He does not appear to have remained in the district for more than a few weeks before moving on to pastures new.

A longer lived, more widespread and more intensive joy riding operation, the precursor of several years of similar activity, was that inaugurated by the civil aircraft operating division of A.V. Roe and Co. from Swansea Sands a little later in the year. Using numerous examples of their most famous product, the Avro 504K biplane, Avro, as the company was generally known, mounted a widespread joy riding operation that encompassed many of Britain's most popular resorts throughout the summer of 1919 and introduced some 30,000 people to flying in the process. One of the most familiar sights in the British skies during the inter-war years, the Avro 504 was designed in 1913 and initially saw service as a bomber, later finding favour as a training aeroplane. Following the armistice, hundreds, mostly 504Ks, were sold as surplus to civil operators who, by dint of enlarging the rear cockpit and installing two seats, converted them into economical joy riding machines. Many more 504Ks remained in RAF service along with the later 504Ns some of which also appeared on the civil register in later years. Powered by various rotary engines, Bentley, Clerget, Gnome and Le Rhône, the Avro was responsible for the aerial baptism of more people than any other aeroplane of that time.

The first Avro machine to visit Swansea arrived on Monday 1 June piloted by Col. G.L.P. Henderson who, having looped before landing, found himself surrounded by a horde of admiring small boys.

The object of his visit was to assess the suitability of the sands as a flying ground and locate a suitable site for offices. As a result, a flying ground was established between Brynmill Arch and Blackpill, where the aeroplanes were kept, office accommodation consisting of two small huts located on the nearby recreation ground.

A varied and eventful season commenced on 26 July when Cllr George Hemmings was taken for a flight 'in the unavoidable absence of the Mayor.' Charges were one guinea for a short flight, two guineas for a fifteen-minute flight with a surcharge of 5s for aerobatics. Business appears to have been reasonably brisk throughout the season with the pilots Capts Bruce and Dalton and Lt Drummond-Wolff flying whenever conditions permitted, even taking advantage of low cloud to give their passengers a view of the cloud from above. The aeroplanes used seem to have varied throughout the season, it being probable that the company interchanged them from time to time. The operation was not confined solely to

Swansea, flying grounds being established at Llanelli Sands and Llandrindod Wells almost immediately. In August it was reported that a new five-seater had arrived and often conveyed picnic parties to Caswell and Rhossili Bays. That was presumably an Avro 536, a variant of the 504K with a slightly widened fuselage that allowed four passengers to be crammed into the rear cockpit. It was also reported in the local press that a Miss Dolly Elsworthy had achieved an unusual 'first' in being the first woman in Wales to fly in a bathing costume.

In August the company extended its sphere of operations to include flying from the grounds of the Abernant Lake Hotel at Llanwrtyd Wells and in order to defray the cost of positioning flights inaugurated what amounted to South Wales' first scheduled air service leaving Swansea at 11.00 a.m. and Llanwrtyd Wells at 7.00 p.m. The inaugural flight departed from Swansea on 11 August piloted by Capt. Bruce but, with a charge of £5 per head return at a time when a day return from Swansea to Ilfracombe by paddle steamer cost 6s, it is hardly surprising that the service was not a success and was abandoned after ten days.

The season was not without incident. One Avro inbound to Swansea crashed while attempting a landing at Lock's Common, Porthcawl, on 16 August without injury to its two occupants. Another, when taking off from Llanelli Sands on 12 September, struck a pony cart that was giving rides to children sadly killing the seventy-four-year-old driver and slightly injuring three of his passengers. Finally on 27 September Capt. Bruce, who was accompanied by a mechanic and a passenger, became lost while proceeding from Swansea to Blackwood sports where he was due to give pleasure flights and in the ensuing precautionary landing at the unattractively named Gwern-y-Domen Farm, near Caerphilly, ran into a wall slightly damaging the aeroplane in the process.

A quite different sight appeared in the South Wales sky on the morning of Monday 7 July in the shape of HM Airship SR.1 on a flight promoting Victory Loan. As her designation implied SR.1 was the first – and only – semi-rigid airship to enter British service. An Italian M-type airship purchased by the Admiralty for evaluation she was quite a large craft for her

HM Airship SR1, *The torpedo-like object just in front of the control cabin is a crew rest bunk. Not an ideal place of repose for the somnambulant.* (Photograph courtesy of the Imperial War Museum, London; negative No.Q66787)

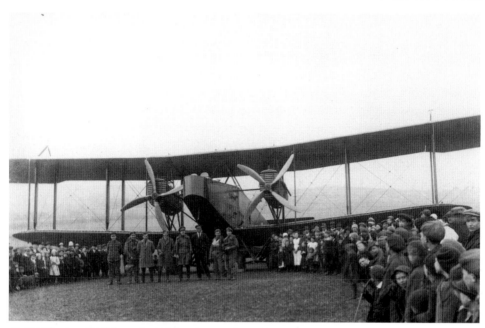

R.H. Thomas (third from the right) and crew of Handley Page 0/400 at Coity Fields, Bridgend, in 1919. (E. Carver & Son, Bridgend)

day. With a length of 269ft and a maximum diameter of 59ft giving her a capacity of 441,000cu.ft, she was much larger than the contemporary non-rigid coastal patrol airships that had become such familiar sights over the coastal waters during the war. First flown on 26 August 1918 with three engines, two Italia, licence-built Maybachs and a single S.P.A. that produced a maximum speed of 45-50mph, she had arrived in the UK on 31 October 1918 following an eventful three and a half day flight from Ciampino, Rome. It was the first aerial journey from Italy to England, a feat that earned her commander, Capt. G.F. Meager, the award of the Air Force Cross. The war ended before SR.1 was ready for active service, her sole contribution being to act as escort to the surrendering German U-boat fleet at Harwich on 20 November 1918. Shortly afterwards the S.P.A engine was removed and she flew on the two Italias only.

On the flight in question she slipped her moorings at Pulham, Norfolk, at 10.10 p.m. on Sunday 6 July under George Meager's command and following a night flight across the Midlands appeared over Cardiff at 7.00 a.m. on the following morning. Her track then took her at low level over Llanishen, Caerphilly, Pontypridd and Aberdare, before a lowering cloudbase near Merthyr Tydfil dictated a change of course along the Neath Valley to Neath. The flight continued to Swansea, Kidwelly and Carmarthen, after which SR.1 returned to Swansea then followed the coast via Port Talbot and Porthcawl to Nash Point to the west of Llantwit Major where she coasted out towards Minehead. She returned to her Pulham mast at 11.30 p.m., having been airborne for twenty-five hours and twenty minutes. It was one of her last flights. Declared surplus to requirements she was deflated on 29 August after an active life of only one year and three days.

Handley Page 0/400 at Coity Fields, Bridgend, in 1919. Note the absence of any form of registration marks. (E. Carver & Son, Bridgend)

Cardiff received a visit from a band of itinerant joy riding pilots on 5 August when three Avro 504Ks operated by Vickers Ltd arrived at Ely Racecourse. Despite the usual charge of one guinea the pilots, Capts Lewis MC, (Cecil Lewis, the author of the Great War aviation classic *Sagittarius Rising*, later to be a founder member of the embryo BBC and an Oscar-winning Hollywood scriptwriter), F.C. Brome DFC and R. Horrocks were kept busy during their visit, many would-be fliers having to be turned away.

Meanwhile, just a few miles to the east, visitors to a fête held in aid of Red Cross funds at the Sophia Gardens were afforded a reminder of the gentle grace of bygone days when on three successive evenings Cardiff's own aeronaut E.T. Willows ascended in an 80,000cu.ft gas balloon. On each occasion, perched on the basket rim was another familiar figure from pre-war days, parachutist Elsa Spencer, by then Mrs Gladys Gooding, the wife of a well-known Queen Street photographer.

Weather conditions were far from ideal when the balloon ascended in the early evening of Tuesday 5 August with Willows, Miss Spencer and two passengers aboard. A northerly wind carried it over Riverside and Grangetown where it was joined by one of Vickers' Avros on a joy flight from Ely. With the sea fast approaching Miss Spencer dropped and, with the Avro circling above her, floated down to alight in the heavily polluted waters of the River Taff near Clarence Road Bridge. Fortunately the tide was out and the bedraggled young woman was able to wade to the bank dragging the parachute behind her. Willows decided to terminate the flight before reaching the coast and valved the balloon down to a safe landing in a field near Penarth.

Near perfect conditions prevailed for the Wednesday evening ascent and no less than six passengers availed themselves of the opportunity to accompany the aeronauts. The balloon took up a south easterly track. When over Butetown Miss Spencer took her leave of it and shortly afterwards found herself in deep water, literally, when her descent terminated in the Roath Basin. A non-swimmer she was somewhat disconcerted to discover that her lifejacket had deflated but the quick thinking crew of a Spanish ship moored nearby launched a boat and effected an efficient rescue. Willows, meanwhile, ascended to 4,800ft and crossed the Bristol Channel to Burcott, near Wells, where he and his companions spent a convivial night in a hotel before returning to Cardiff next day.

Willows' final ascent was something of a family occasion, his sister Dorthy and his eight-year-old-son Clifford being among the passengers. It must have come as quite a relief to Elsa Spencer to discover that the wind had swung to the south thereby ensuring a descent on terra firma. After her departure to a safe landing in the vicinity of Llandaff Fields the balloon continued to the north until approaching the Rhondda Valley where Willows found a northerly wind that carried it over Barry and the Bristol Channel to a moonlight landing at 3.00 a.m. at Dotheridge, near Clovelly. Not one to spare his father's blushes young Clifford when asked for his impressions said, 'I didn't like the landing, we bumped so.'

Willows never flew from Cardiff again. A bitter man as a result of what he perceived to be official indifference to his achievements he spent the remainder of his life in the London area where he embarked on various ventures that led to his financial ruin. He worked at one time as an unqualified marine engineer and also, as Capt. Willows, piloted balloons on an occasional basis for Messrs C.G. Spencer & Sons. While so employed he was killed along with his four passengers in an accident to a tethered joy riding balloon at Kempston, near Bedford, on 3 August 1926. His father, whose entrepreneurial instincts had also proved to be disastrous, died an undischarged bankrupt on 19 October 1931, only fifteen days after William Beedle.

A national strike by some 500,000 railway workers that lasted from 26 September to 5 October brought chaos to the country, whose system of long-distance road transport had hardly begun to develop, forcing the government to take emergency measures that included the rationining of some foodstuffs and the commandeering of vehicles, and provided an opportunity to demonstrate the utility of the aeroplane as a fast, if expensive, means of communication. Obviously neither the Royal Air Force nor the combined fleets of the civil air operators possessed the capability to move more than a very few passengers but aeroplanes proved their worth in distributing government mail, vital documents and, in those days before public broadcasting, news.

Throughout the strike aeroplanes, both military and civil, criss-crossed the country, the RAF carrying mostly government mail while the civil operators carried vital documents, newspapers and a few passengers. Among the civil operators, the Avro company were particularly prominent having some fifty aeroplanes available at the end of the summer joy riding season and they used them to the full.

The first load of Sunday newspapers arrived at Pontcanna Farm, Cardiff, at 9.30 a.m. on Sunday 28 September and throughout the strike the Avro company maintained a regular newspaper service from Hounslow to Cardiff and Swansea Sands. It was estimated that the cost per newspaper, of which several tons were delivered, worked out at 1s 2d but, nevertheless, they still retailed at 1d per copy. Only one passenger was reported to have been carried, an unnamed Swansea businessman who flew to keep an appointment in Chepstow.

The RAF commenced a mail service to South Wales on Monday 29 September using Avro 504Ks which flew daily from RAF Stonehenge, Wiltshire, to Pembroke Dock. No intermediate landings were made, the mailbags being simply dropped from very low level onto the then wide open space of Cardiff Arms Park and an unspecified site at Swansea from where they were delivered to their addressees by police officers on bicycles. The RAF technique was emulated by an unidentified civil aviator who caused considerable public alarm on 1 October when flying just above rooftop level he dropped a parcel into Roath Park, Cardiff. It was reported that on 3 October the RAF crew succeeded in depositing a mailbag in the narrow confines of the courtyard of The Angel Hotel, Westgate Street, Cardiff, just across the road from the Arms Park, whether that was a feat of exceptional skill or an abysmal failure to hit the hallowed turf of the Arms Park I know not. The RAF service ended dramatically on 6 October, the day that the strikers returned to work, when fuel shortage on the final stage of the journey from Swansea to Pembroke Dock obliged the pilot, Lt Lloyd, to attempt a precautionary landing in a field adjacent to Llanelli Steelworks, in the course of which the aeroplane was badly damaged. Lloyd and his observer, Lt Thompson, were unhurt and returned to Stonehenge along with their damaged aeroplane – by train!

On Monday 13 October, a small group of people braved the chilly morning wind that swept across the fields of Sweldon Farm to the west of Cardiff's Ely Racecourse in order to witness an event that, unbeknown to them, was to be a significant milestone in the history of British civil aviation, the inauguration of a private airmail service linking Cardiff, London and Paris by the Cardiff-based shipping line S. Instone & Co. Among the group was the company's energetic and innovative chairman, Samuel Instone. Born Samuel Einstein at Gravesend, Kent, in 1878, a distant relative of the physicist Albert, he commenced his lifetime career in shipping and allied industries when he joined the French Compagnie Maritime Boulognaise at the age of fifteen. He progressed rapidly and in 1899 was appointed manager of the company's Cardiff office. Five years later he resigned and together with his brother, Theodore, founded the company that bore his name. From small beginnings, the company went from strength to strength until by the time of the armistice it owned or operated thirty-eight vessels.

It was during the war when anti-German feeling reached such heights of madness that even pet dachshunds were reportedly put to death, yet British troops continued to fight and die in uniforms whose khaki dye had been manufactured in Germany and imported clandestinely via neutral states, that the Einsteins in common with many others, deemed it prudent to renounce their Germanic surname in favour of an anglicised alternative and so the name of the family and the firm was changed to Instone.

The return of peace did not bring plane sailing to the shipping industry. Among the problems that plagued many companies, Instones included, was the virtual collapse of continental postal and telegraph services. It was quite common for ships to lie at anchor off the north French ports for up to ten days awaiting the arrival of documents from the United Kingdom without which they were unable to dock and discharge their cargoes. The cost in charter fees and demurrage was crippling.

The Instone board hit upon a novel solution to the problem. Why not use an aeroplane to transport documentation from the company's Cardiff and London offices to France? The high cost of the operation would be far outweighed by the saving in time and money that it would produce. Samuel Instone, who had always visualised the potential of air transport since he had backed E.T. Willows' endeavours in 1910, was enthusiastic and negotiations with the GPO and the civil aviation department of the Air Ministry commenced in June.

Permission to operate the service was readily obtained, as was much useful advice on the choice of aeroplane and pilot. As a result a government surplus, but unused, Airco D.H.4 powered by a 350hp Rolls-Royce Eagle VIII engine was purchased and a pilot, Lt F.L. Barnard AFC, employed. Franklin Leslie Barnard had been a flying enthusiast since childhood when, so the story goes, he had had some small involvement with the well-known aviation pioneer S.F. Cody. The Great War had afforded him the opportunity to learn to fly and at the cessation of hostilities he was serving as a pilot with No.24 (communications) squadron engaged largely in ferrying VIPs to and from the Continent, just the sort of experience that Instones required. All that was needed was an airfield for the Cardiff end of the operation and the decision was taken to lease land at Sweldon Farm, Ely, long since covered by the housing development between Cowbridge Road West and the Ely Link Road.

The inaugural flight on 13 October commenced at 8.30 a.m., the aeroplane bearing its newly allocated civil registration G-EAMU and the name *City of Cardiff* having been positioned from London to Cardiff the previous evening. Mrs Instone handed Barnard a letter from the Cardiff Chamber of Commerce to the Paris Chamber of Commerce and without more ado he and his mechanic, Mr Oldfield, took off, gave a brief aerobatic display, and set course for the Hounslow airfield, London, which they reached in fifty-six minutes. An hour later they left for Le Bourget airfield, Paris, where they landed after a flight of one hour fifty-five minutes, having dropped leaflets over the company's office at Boulogne en route.

The service, which was also occasionally used to transport company personnel, appears to have been short lived, presumably being discontinued when the postal services returned to normal, but is significant in that it was the beginning of major aviation developments by the Instone Co. In 1920, they acquired a Bristol Tourer capable of carrying a pilot and two passengers with which they undertook light charter work mostly from Croydon. From those small beginnings evolved the Instone Airline of which Sir Samuel Instone, as he had by then become, was chairman and F.L. Barnard chief pilot. Its fleet of eleven aeroplanes, based at Croydon, operated scheduled continental services outside the scope of this story until the company's assets were acquired by the newly formed government-owned Imperial Airways Ltd, of which Sir Samuel became a director and F.L. Barnard chief pilot. The Instone airmail service was in fact the first of two small Cardiff-based air transport operations that developed to form major components of the present national carrier British Airways.

The D.H.4 G-EAMU converted to D.H.4A standard with a coupé rear cockpit and renamed *City of York* achieved further distinction as a racing aeroplane when it won the first King's Cup Air Race in 1922 for Sir Samuel Instone piloted by F.L. Barnard. Sadly, Barnard's hobby of air racing was to prove his undoing. He was killed on 28 July 1927 near Filton, Bristol, while carrying out an air test on the Bristol Badminton aeroplane that he was due to fly in that year's King's Cup Air Race.

11

The Barnstorming Years, 1920-1930

Parodoxical is a word frequently used by economists and social historians to describe the situation that prevailed during the inter-war years. The short-term consumer boom resulting from the dissipation of service gratuities and cashed-in war savings ended abruptly in April 1921 and only then did the penalty that Britain had paid for its war effort become fully apparent. The direction of industrial effort to the production of munitions and other artefacts of war at the expense of supplying overseas markets had led Britain's former trading partners to forge links with non-combatant nations, links that remained intact after the cessation of hostilities. With overseas trade severely depleted, industries such as coal, iron and steel, heavy engineering, ship building, shipping and textiles experienced a steep decline resulting in unemployment and misery for millions who lived in the areas on which those industries were centred – South Wales being no exception.

Meanwhile the country as a whole enjoyed two decades of sustained economic growth. New industries based largely on the mass production of motor vehicles and domestic consumer goods proliferated in the Midlands and south east of England providing a relatively prosperous living for most of the eighty per cent of the population unaffected by the scourge of unemployment. Taxation had yet to take its toll on the wealthy while skilled artisans and members of the burgeoning white-collar class enjoyed previously unimagined prosperity.

Many were able to leave their town centre domiciles for a healthier life in the expanding leafy suburbs, their lives changed for the better by the availability of inexpensive domestic appliances, the cinema and the commencement of public service broadcasting, while small affordable motor cars and motorcycles provided mobility previously undreamed of.

Aviation generally did not flourish during the 1920s. The RAF contracted to a fraction of its wartime strength while commercial aviation ventures were beset with difficulties. The only British airline services between London and the Continent failed to prosper. The pioneering company Aircraft Transport & Travel ceased trading in December 1920 and the remaining three, Daimler Airway, Instone Airline and Handley Page Transport, despite belated government subsidies, finally abandoned the unequal struggle of competing against heavily subsidised foreign operators and, along with the more recently formed British Marine Air Navigation Co., merged to form the embryo Imperial Airways, a wholly state-owned organisation on 31 March 1924.

The remainder of the commercial aviation was largely undertaken by the few small joy riding and charter companies that survived the ending of the post-war boom but the days of the guinea-a-head joy flight soon ended. The lack of a suitably economic, purpose-built aircraft type precluded any attempts at internal airline operations.

The same can be said of private flying in the early part of the decade, only surplus military aeroplanes being available to the handful of private fliers in the country. A laudable attempt by the *Daily Mail* to rectify the situation and bring aviation within the means of the 'man in the street' led to the *Daily Mail* Light Aeroplane Trials of 1923 and 1924. Although well supported by most aircraft manufacturers, the stipulated restrictions on size and power resulted in a plethora of prototypes so underpowered that most could only be coaxed into the air and kept there by pilots of exceptional skill.

It was not until 1925 when Capt. Geoffrey de Havilland, a competitor in the Daily Mail trials, realised the futility of attempting to design a people's aeroplane utilising contemporary technology and produced a compromise, that light aviation became a practical proposition. A robust two-seater biplane retailing at £600, about the same price as a suburban semi-detached house, the D.H.60 Moth, although beyond the means of the majority of the population, sold in large numbers both to private owners and the emergent flying club movement. It was the first of a long line of De Havilland light aeroplanes built between the wars and inspired other manufacturers to follow De Havilland's example, resulting as time went on in a British light aeroplane industry second to none.

As the reader will no doubt have surmised, aviation activity in Glamorgan reached a low ebb during the period in question, being confined to the activities of barnstorming pilots based either locally or elsewhere and a mere handful of interesting visitors.

Barnstormer, originally a transatlantic term for an itinerant rural entertainer, was an appellation frequently applied to that small band of aviators who earned their living by touring the land during the summer months offering joy rides to the public. They fell into two basic groups - those who operated from a number of fixed sites, usually at seaside resorts and those who roamed the length and breadth of the country flying for short periods from rented farmers' fields before moving on, quite literally, to pastures new.

The Swansea-based Avro operation recommenced for the summer season of 1920 on 1 May, operated under licence by Capts E.A. Sullock and F.G.M. Sparkes, who appear to have flown from the same sites as the previous year with the exception of Llanwrtyd Wells, the minimum charge, for a six-mile flight, being £1.

The only opportunity for residents of the eastern part of the county to experience the joys of flight came when Lt A.R. Van Den Burgh's Avro 504K G-EATB, piloted by Lt F. Neale, visited Ely Racecourse, Cardiff, between 7 and 29 August and Holton Farm, Barry, flying from a site now bounded by Jenner Road, Colcot Road and Claude Road from 30 August to 12 September. Business at Cardiff was brisk from the start but on arrival at Barry Van Den Burgh found an air of trepidation among those assembled at the flying field. He overcame the problem by offering a free flight to two police constables in attendance. When those worthies returned smiling to the ground he found no shortage of patrons eager to pay the traditional guinea to view their town from aloft or to pay a small additional fee to experience the delight (or horror) of looping the loop.

The arrangements between Capts Sullock and Sparkes and Messrs A.V. Roe are now lost in the mists of time but were apparently severed at the end of the 1920 season. Whatever transpired prompted the two aviators along with four local backers to form the Welsh Aviation Co., which was registered in December 1920 with a registered office at 31 Fisher Street, Swansea, and a capital of £5,000 in £5 shares.

The company operated during the 1921 season using four aeroplanes, Avro 548 G-EAFH powered by an 80hp Renault engine and three Avro 504Ks G-EAWK, G-EAWL and G-EAWM, all powered by 110hp Le Rhône engines. The fleet was supplemented by a civilianised Sopwith Camel Fighter G-EAWN (130hp Clerget), the property of one of the company's pilots Capt. Hubert Broad who gave aerobatic displays at Swansea and Lock's Common.

The Welsh Aviation Co. appears to have accounted for virtually all aerial activity in the county during the year 1921. The only other reports were of the passage of HM Airship R.36 up the Bristol Channel on 11 January, of which more anon, and a court case in July in which E.D.C. Herne was fined for flying from London to Cardiff, landing site not stated, in an aeroplane that had not been subjected to the requisite daily inspection.

In September, Capt. Sparkes took a short busman's holiday when he flew to Croydon to compete in the first Croydon Aviation Meeting on the 17th. Flying the Avro 548 he swept the board winning the Club Handicap, Croydon Handicap and Autumn Handicap races.

Sadly, in common with so many of its contemporaries, the Welsh Aviation Co. failed to weather the economic downturn of 1921 and in February 1922 at the Garage, Norton Road, West Cross, Swansea, Messrs, Clarke Davey & Co. auctioned its fleet to satisfy an execution issued by the Bailiff of the Liberties of Gower and Kilvey against it. Bidding was far from brisk, the entire fleet being knocked down to Mr Evan Williams, a Llanelli commission agent and qualified pilot, for a derisory sum. The Avro 504s fetched £50, £40 and £30 while the Avro 548 changed hands for a mere £12 10s. Capt. Sullock apparently re-joined the RAF, while Sparky Sparkes went on to become one of the legendary figures of the early days of the British flying club movement before emigrating to Canada where he was killed in a flying accident in 1928.

Having disposed of the Avro 548 to Dr Douglas Whitehead Reid, a well-known amateur pilot of the time, Evan Williams in partnership with Mr Bush, a prominent rubber merchant, commenced a joy riding operation during the summer of 1922. They used the three Avro 504s and ranged from Porthcawl to Tenby, the flying being shared between Williams and

Capt. Hubert Broad of the Welsh Aviation Co, in Sopwith Camel G-EAWN in Swansea Sands, 1921. (Author's collection)

Bush's son, Percy. With the exception of a minor landing accident to Evan Williams at Lock's Common in September, the operation seems to have been quite uneventful until 2 October when Percy Bush, Evan Williams and a friend, Sgt-Maj. J.S.H. Biggins RASC, stationed at Swansea Drill Hall, decided to take an end of season trip around the district in G-EAWK. On returning to the sands they apparently found that the tide had risen rather faster than expected and Bush, who was at the controls, tightened his turn onto the final approach path in order to land on the remaining dry sand. In so doing he inadvertently stalled the aeroplane which spun from low level into shallow water. Despite Herculean efforts by the would-be rescuers who rushed to their aid all three men were dead when extracted from the wreckage.

The accident, which at a stroke extinguished its two leading lights, put local aviation into a state of eclipse that endured for several years.

The paucity of aerial activity in the district can be gauged from the following extracts from *The Barry Dock News*. The edition of 1 December 1922 proclaimed: 'An infrequent visitor since the war, an aeroplane flew over the *Barry Dock News* offices on Wednesday morning of this week.' On 8 June 1923 the same journal reported that: 'The first aeroplane in Barry this year flew at very low altitude over the town.' Two attempts to set up air transport undertakings during 1924, a seaplane service between Mount Stuart Dry Dock and Weston-super-Mare, and a landplane service between Plymouth, Cardiff, Birmingham and Manchester, failed to reach fruition as did an attempt the same year to establish a flying club at Cardiff.

The flying club movement came into being as a result of a government initiative, intended to encourage airmindedness, announced in August 1924, whereby organisations able to convince the Air Ministry as to their suitability to operate a viable flying club received a con-

Capt. F.G.M. Sparkes, with a little help from his ground crew, running up the engine of an Avro 504 of the Welsh Aviation Co. at Swansea Sands in the summer of 1921. (Author's collection)

siderable subsidy. The scheme provided for a grant of £2,000 on formation, £500 per annum for the following two years plus £10 for each 'A' licence, the equivalent of today's Private Pilot's Licence, gained. The appearance the following year of the D.H.60 Moth, an ideal club training aeroplane, ensured the movement's success.

Despite the subsidies, the cost of flying remained high. Hourly rates, typically £2 per hour – the best part of a working man's weekly wage – confined club membership to the ranks of the well-to-do. Nevertheless, the scheme was an outstanding success. From small beginnings in 1925 when the first five participating clubs enrolled 780 members, flew 727 hours and trained just twelve pilots, the movement expanded rapidly until by 1928 thirteen clubs whose total membership was approaching 5,000 flew 12,201 hours and trained 475 pilots. The movement continued to expand until the outbreak of the Second World War, although it was to be some time before such facilities were to be provided in Glamorgan.

The General Strike that commenced at midnight on 3 May 1926 produced a situation reminiscent of the 1919 railway strike and once again aeroplanes were used to good effect in keeping open essential lines of communication during the nine days of chaos that ensued. As before, the RAF was charged with the responsibility of distributing essential government mail whilst the Royal Aero Club co-ordinated the activities of ten civil operators whose combined fleet of twenty-five aircraft covered 44,733 miles distributing such newspapers as were available along with other essential items to all parts of the Kingdom.

In the east of the county the RAF established a temporary airfield at Pentrebane Farm, St Fagans, near Cardiff, under the command of Flt Lt Browning MC. The first arrival, an Avro 504 piloted by Flg-Off. R.E. Bain, touched down after a flight from Filton, near Bristol, on 4 May. The mail was sorted on site and distributed to all parts of Glamorgan and Monmouthshire by police motorcyclists from the Glamorgan, Cardiff City and Newport Borough Forces, aided by some civilian volunteers. As can be imagined, Swansea Sands once more played host to a variety of visiting civil aeroplanes.

It is now an opportune time in the story to introduce three personalities who in their different ways played major roles in local aviation history from the mid-1920s until the outbreak of the Second World War.

The first, Sir Alan Cobham, a former RFC and RAF pilot turned post-war barnstormer was a household name as a result of a series of long distance return flights to Rangoon, Capetown and Adelaide between 1924 and 1926, for which achievements he had been knighted. An astute businessman, he had in 1927 founded Alan Cobham Aviation Ltd, aerodrome consultants, aerodrome experts and air route surveyors, the objective being to convince local authorities of the potential of aviation as a means of communication and persuade them to construct municipal aerodromes that would be managed by the company. By dint of a series of lecture tours and appearances at local functions, Sir Alan was moderately successful in the first aim, a considerable number of municipal aerodromes were opened in the following decade, but less successful in the latter intention as most local authorities elected to manage their own affairs.

The other two, both local men, were disparate characters: Capt. W.R. Bailey and Mr R.H. Thomas.

William Richardson Bailey, his title of captain derived from part-time service with the Gloucestershsire Hussars, was the youngest son of Mr C.H. Bailey of the well-known ship repairing firm of Bailey Graham. He was a young man whose considerable private means and ample leisure time allowed him to indulge his passions for golf, flying and riding to hounds to the full. His first involvement with flying, it is said, came about during the First World War when, concealing the fact that he was only sixteen years old, he had joined the RFC and commenced flying training. However, his guilty secret came to light and his service career terminated. He continued to fly after the war and was awarded Aviator's Certificate No.7905 on 17 November 1920. He remained an enthusiastic and dynamic member of the South Wales flying fraternity during the inter-war years, despite receiving serious injuries when his Avro 504K G-EBCL crashed at Rogerstone, near Newport, on 6 May 1922.

By contrast, Bob Thomas was a self-made man. A former member of the Royal Naval Air Service, his first appearance on the South Wales aviation scene had been as a member of the crew of a Handley Page 0/400 bomber that had landed at Coity Fields near his native Bridgend during the course of a round-Britain navigation exercise in 1919. Although the landing does not appear to be recorded in print, it is well remembered locally and photographic evidence by a local photographer is contained in these pages. After the war Bob Thomas entered the garage business in Bridgend and, in the words of his brother-in-law, the late Mr Joe Morgan, made a great deal of money most of which he spent on aeroplanes.

Robert Thomas's activities commenced in the spring of 1927 when he formed South Wales Airways Ltd, based in a field at Laleston, near Bridgend. The company operated a number of government surplus Avro 504Ks on joy riding and charter work although Thomas also harboured ambitions of forming a government-supported flying club.

Joe Morgan, for many years the company's engineer, recalled in conversation with the author how the aeroplanes, with their wings removed, were towed tail first behind motor cars from a storage depot at RAF Manston Kent to Bridgend where they were re-assembled and refurbished to three-seater joy riding configuration using, among other things, plywood from tea chests to form the non load-bearing fuselage upper decking.

The company's first year of operation was attended by one mishap. One of the Avros piloted by Capt. Bannister came to grief on 23 June when attempting to take off with a full load from a field at Carrig Croes farm, Llanyre, Radnorshire. After several aborted attempts to get airborne in the distance available the aeroplane finally struck the far hedge, narrowly missing a passing car, before hitting the hedge at the far side of the adjoining road, damaging the engine, propeller and the legs of the unfortunate pilot. The passengers, however, escaped injury.

Unlike many of its contemporaries, South Wales Airways remained solvent and its aeroplanes became a familiar sight joy riding from Swansea Sands, Lock's Common and Llwydcoed, near Aberdare, where they flew from the field immediately to the south of the junction of the road from Llwydcoed and the old Hirwaun to Merthyr road near the Cross Bychan public house for the remainder of the inter-war years.

Also a familiar sight during the early summer months of 1927 and 1928 were the pale blue Avros of the well-known Croydon-based company Surrey Flying Services on their annual barnstorming tours. They flew at various times from: Pentrebane Farm, St Fagans, near Cardiff; Cogan Hall Farm, Penarth; a field behind the Colcot Arms public house, Barry; a field on the opposite side of the A48 to the Old Post Office, Margam; and Cimla Racecourse, Neath, a site now covered by housing. Surrey Flying Services' operations were not without incident. While returning to his temporary base at Margam after a day's flying at Neath, Capt. A.F. Muir, the firm's chief pilot, crashed into a field near Old Park Farm on 31 May 1927, wrecking the aeroplane and sustaining injuries to his wrist, legs and nose. Muir came to grief again the following year on Whit Monday 28 May 1928 when taking off with two passengers in an easterly direction on a hot and windless afternoon from the field behind the Colcot Arms, Barry. The Avro barely cleared Port Road, which was heavily congested with traffic, headed for the local beaches, struck some telephone wires and the roof of Gordon House, a bungalow now 86 Port Road, in whose garden it came to rest badly damaged and festooned in the household's washing. Damage to the bungalow was confined to some broken slates and crockery dislodged from a dresser by the force of the impact. The householder, Mr W.J. Simpkins and his wife were unhurt as was their three-year-old niece, Pat Roach, who was playing in the garden at the time. Capt. Muir was only slightly injured and his passengers, a young couple, 'clambered out as soon as the 'plane struck the ground and rushing across the ground were not seen again.'

It was a Surrey Flying Services Avro that landed in a field adjoining Ely Racecourse, Cardiff, carrying a jockey, C. Rhodes, who had missed his train from London and nearly his booking to ride two of Lord Glanely's horses at the Cardiff Easter Meeting of 1927. Despite arriving in ample time, his journey was in vain, neither of his mounts being placed.

On 13 May 1927, Capt. W.R. Bailey, then resident in the London area, took delivery of a new D.H. 60 Moth G-EBQY powered by an A.D.C. Cirrus II engine which he based at the De Havilland Aerodrome at Stag Lane, Edgeware. He used the aeroplane on a number of occasions to visit South Wales, usually landing at the Royal Porthcawl Golf Club of which he was a member. On one occasion he broke his return journey in order to take tea with his father's business partner, Sir William Graham of Friar's Point House, Barry. Having circled the area for about ten minutes and dropped a red flare to signify his intention, he landed the Moth on the sands of Whitmore Bay, taxied up to the sea wall and left it with its wings folded in the charge of a police constable while he walked the few hundred yards to Friar's Point House.

However, landing facilities were not always so readily available and the following November he reluctantly disposed of the aeroplane complaining bitterly to that effect. Yet things were beginning to change, albeit slowly. In May of 1927 Sir Alan Cobham had visited both Cardiff and Swansea by surface transport in the course of a lecture tour designed to promote his municipal aerodrome scheme and, undoubtedly, in Cardiff at least, the first seeds of interest were sown.

The year 1928 was notable only for two spectacular accidents and a number of interesting visitors. On 7 May Ronald Matthews, a pilot newly employed by South Wales Airways, took off on his first flight with the company in order to familiarise himself with the local area. Shortly afterwards the aeroplane, Avro 504K G-EBNH, crashed whilst attempting a forced landing in a field belonging to Park Farm at the rear of Park Street, Bridgend, and was 'smashed to match wood'. Matthews managed to extricate himself from the wreckage and was subsequently removed from the scene hunting field fashion on a five-barred gate at the commencement of his journey to Bridgend Cottage Hospital. Capt. Muir's Barry accident occurred only three weeks later.

Great excitement prevailed among the local populace when it was learned that Sir Alan Cobham would visit Cardiff by air on Sunday 10 June 1928, piloting the Short S.5 Singapore flying boat G-EBUP in which he and his crew had recently returned from a much publicised six-month, 20,000-mile survey flight around Africa. Powered by two 650hp Rolls-Royce

Condor III A engines and having an all up weight of 20,000lb and a top speed of 128mph, the Singapore was considered to be a very advanced aeroplane at the time.

Despite windy weather and rough seas a large crowd congregated along Penarth seafront to await Sir Alan's arrival while the Lord Mayor of Cardiff and other local dignitaries put to sea aboard a pilot cutter to welcome him. Shortly after 11.00 a.m. the silver and white flying boat appeared from the direction of Lavernock Point and proceeded to circle Cardiff and Penarth before setting up an approach to alight in front of Penarth promenade. However, deterred by the state of the sea, Sir Alan decided to go around and, to the disappointment of the spectators, alighted on the more sheltered waters in the lee of Penarth Head where the civic party eventually caught up with him.

Sir Alan and Lady Cobham, his co-pilot Capt. H.V. Worral DSC and Gen. Groves, secretary of the Air League of the British Empire, and his wife were then conveyed via Cardiff Pier Head to the Mansion House where, in a post luncheon speech, Sir Alan once more seized the opportunity to promote his municipal aerodrome scheme. Later the Singapore was towed to a point off Penarth where the party with the exception of Capt. Worral, who had been stricken with a bout of recurrent malaria, re-embarked. After take-off Sir Alan brought the Singapore low along Penarth seafront before turning and climbing away towards the Somerset coast.

Scarcely a week elapsed before a young and unknown American social worker by the name of Amelia Earhart became the first woman to cross the Atlantic by air when, in the course of 17 and 18 June she travelled as a passenger in the Fokker F.VIIB/3M Trimotor floatplane *Friendship*, commanded by Wilmer Stultz and crewed by Lincoln Ellsworthy and Louis Gordon from Trepassy Bay, Newfoundland, to Burry Port. The event caused great excitement both locally and internationally and brought a number of chartered aeroplanes carrying London news hounds to Swansea Sands. Another, a small blue biplane, probably a Surrey Flying Services Avro, whose pilot had been instructed to fly to 'Barry Port', landed on the sands of Whitmore Bay, Barry Island. After an animated conversation with a beach inspector and the inevitable police constable the pilot was re-directed and continued his journey westward towards Swansea.

The *South Wales Weekly Mail* of 18 May reported the departure from Cardiff by air of the well-known Australian speedway rider Smoky Stratton who was thereby able to ride at both the Welsh White City track at Sloper Road and Sheffield on the same day. He was conveyed in an Avro 504 of Northern Airlines of Manchester. Stratton's departure point was not reported but at that time it could have been from any convenient field as no recognised landing facility existed. However, events later in the year and during 1930 began to point the way to aviation's coming of age in the Cardiff area.

Sir Alan Cobham returned to Cardiff on 31 August 1929 at the controls of his D.H.61 Giant Moth biplane G-AAEV *Youth of Britain* as part of a nation-wide tour to promote his municipal aerodrome scheme. A reasonably large aeroplane the D.H.61 was powered by a 500hp Armstrong Siddeley Jaguar VIC engine, had a wingspan of 52ft and an all up weight of 7,000lb, allowing it to lift ten passengers in an enclosed cabin ahead of the pilot's open cockpit. During the tour, Sir Alan visited most major towns and cities, flew some 3,500 civic dignitaries and, thanks to sponsorship from Sir Charles Wakefield of Castrol Ltd, 10,000 school children as well.

The most significant factor of Sir Alan's visit was his choice of landing ground – Splott Tidefields at East Moors – the first recorded use of the area by an aeroplane. The visit had

The last of the barnstormers – D.H.60X Moth G-EBOS at Swansea Sands, June 1930. (Author's collection)

the desired effect of stimulating debate on the subject of securing a site for a municipal aerodrome in Cardiff and establishing a flying club and by December of that year the Cardiff City Council had agreed in principle to the acquisition of 770 acres of ground at Splott Tidefields from the Tredegar Estate and others at a cost of £29,000 for the purpose. The decision to site the aerodrome on the foreshore was partly influenced by the anticipated need to cater for marine as well as land-based aircraft.

The aerodrome clause was approved by parliament on 19 March 1930 and it was decided that the levelling of the land and the construction of a sea wall to protect the site from inundation by high tides form part of an unemployment relief scheme.

The proposed site received the Royal seal of approval during the summer of 1930 with two visits from HRH the Prince of Wales, an enthusiastic aviator, who had taken to travelling to official engagements by air whenever possible as a result of which two Westland Wapiti 1A aeroplanes J9095 and J9096 had been allocated to No.24 (communications) squadron RAF specifically for Royal use. On 12 May one of the Wapiti's piloted by Sqn Ldr D.S. Don MVO landed at East Moors to check the suitability of the site prior to the first of the Prince's visits which took place on 21 May. Piloted by Sqn Ldr Don, His Royal Highness arrived to open the Tatem Physics Laboratory at The University College of South Wales and Monmouthshire to the plaudits of a crowd estimated at 15,000 that had assembled to greet him as he emerged from the open cockpit in full flying kit. His equerry Capt. J.R. Aird arrived in the second Wapiti piloted by Flg-Off. Pearson-Rogers. The second visit, to participate in the annual congress of the British Legion, took place on 8 June when a crowd estimated to be 20,000 strong arrived to witness the two Wapitis arrive flying in close formation.

The East Moors site was also being used at that time by the well-known joy riding company Berkshire Aviation Tours using a single 110hp Le Rhône-powered Avro 504K. It was

Desoutter I of Phillips & Powis at Swansea Sands, June 1930.

piloted by Capt. Kingswell who suffered a minor incident, with no resultant damage or injury, caused by engine failure on 9 May. He was also engaged in joy riding from Laleston between 12 and 25 June, the Colcot Arms field at Barry between 10 and 23 July and, although no documentary evidence exits, only word of mouth reminiscences, he probably flew from The Patch, near The Queens Head public house, Pen-y-Coedcae, Pontypridd, at about that time.

Also during that summer, between 5 and 14 June, National Flying services operated a Desoutter I high wing monoplane on joy riding operations from Swansea Sands along with a D.H.60X Moth of Phillips and Powis Ltd of Reading which seemed to be operating under a common banner.

The above named companies were effectively the last examples of independent barnstorming operators of the itinerant kind to appear in the county. Presumably the market had been saturated and falling demand was reflected in the prices charged, usually 5s or less per head.

Realising their declining appeal many independent joy riding companies resolved their difficulties by combining to form the flying circuses that became such a familiar part of the British aviation scene during the first half of the 1930s.

Other branches of aviation also underwent significant changes in the course of the following few years. The opening of new aerodromes gave added impetus to the flying club movement and private aircraft ownership. They were also of immense benefit to the air transport industry as was the introduction in 1932 of the D.H.84 Dragon, a twin-engine biplane capable of carrying eight passengers on only 260hp. The Dragon rendered internal and short range Continental air services financially viable and formed the backbone of commercial aviation until the outbreak of war, the lead up to which was also responsible for a massive upsurge in military aviation.

12

Triumphs and Disasters, 1931

As the fourth decade of the century began it appeared that at last the aspirations and efforts of local aviation enthusiasts had finally begun to cohere and that properly organised aviation had become a reality in the locality.

In January 1931, the formation of Welsh Airways Ltd was announced with joint managing directors, P. Carpenter and T. Jenkins, both of Cardiff. The company's objectives were to establish an aerodrome and flying club in the Cardiff area, an undertaking that was accomplished with startling rapidity. Land was leased from the Wenvoe Estate and Cardiff's first aerodrome, at St Lythan's Down, the field currently occupied by the Wenvoe television mast, received Air Ministry approval before the end of the month. Meanwhile the Cardiff Flying Club had been formed and commenced operations almost immediately. The club fleet consisted of three aeroplanes, an Avro 594 Avian IIIA, G-EBYO, and two Avro 504Ks, G-ABGI and G-ABGJ, the latter of which had no certificate of airworthiness and in fact it is doubtful if either 504K was ever used. The entire fleet was registered in the name of Mrs V. Brailey, wife of the club secretary, E.A. Brailey.

Meanwhile across the city, many previously unemployed men were working under the supervision of Mr G.H. Whitaker, the city engineer on the £18,000 project of constructing a sea wall and draining and levelling the site of the new municipal aerodrome. Curiously Cardiff City Council, although pursuing the project with great enthusiasm, appeared to have given little thought to the management of the completed project. An approach by National Flying Services of Hanworth who already managed six aerodromes and flying clubs across the country was rejected, a wise decision as it turned out, as the company subsequently went out of business.

Ely racecourse played host to the two-aeroplane fleet of Aviation Tours Ltd from 27 April to 3 May. The organisation was in effect halfway between an old-time barnstorming operation and a flying circus which in later years, as will be seen, operated under the banner of Sir Alan Cobham's National Aviation Day Display. Based at London's Croydon Airport its fleet consisted of a Handley Page W.8.b airliner, G-EBBI, *Prince Henry*, leased from Imperial Airways Ltd, piloted by Capt. E.B. Fielden, and an Avro 504K, G-EBYW, in the hands of Capt. H. Lawson, formerly of Berkshire Aviation Tours Ltd. *Prince Henry*, then nearing the end of its active life, had entered service with Handley Page Air Transport in 1922 prior to that company's merger into Imperial Airways with whom it had given yeoman service until declared surplus to requirements in 1931. Converted from its original twelve-seater configuration to a fourteen-seater it became the first airliner to be used as a joy riding machine until finally withdrawn from use in October 1932.

Besides offering flights to the public who paid 5s, 7s 6d, or 10s for the experience of flying in *Prince Henry* (depending on the length of flight), or 10s for a flight in the Avro, those who paid 6d admission charge were entertained to aerobatic displays by Capt. Lawson in the Avro which was also used to carry aloft Pat O'Hara, a former Stamford Bridge and West Ham speedway rider turned wing-walker and parachutist. On the opening day of the visit, Fielden piloted the Lord Mayor and a party of councillors and journalists over the city and an aerial photograph of the city centre taken by a *Western Mail* photographer was subsequently presented to the Council.

Following its Cardiff performances, the group of fliers left for Coventry where on 10 May, following an otherwise successful parachute descent, Pat O'Hara landed facing into wind and overbalanced backwards. Despite the apparent simplicity of his fall he sustained serious brain damage and, like Viola Spencer twenty-one years previously, died in the Coventy and Warwickshire Hospital the following day. The event was rendered all the more ironic by the fact that the display was being given in aid of the funds of that very hospital. Lawson too was killed less than two years later when flying an Avro Tutor during a display with Sir Alan Cobham's circus in Capetown.

Bridgend went en fête between 9 and 16 May to celebrate Empire Shopping Week and due to the energies of Bob Thomas the celebrations involved a considerable aerial content centred on the flying ground at Coity Fields. Events included a fly-past on the opening day by seven Westland Wapiti bombers of 501 (City of Bristol) squadron led by their commanding officer Sqn Ldr R.S. Sugden who broke away from the formation and thrilled the crowd with a low pass over the fields. During the course of the week people were able to try their hand at flying what appears to have been a rudimentary form of flight simulator installed in Bob Thomas's garage or take to the air on joy rides from Coity Fields.

About a dozen pilots, mostly well-known names, flying a variety of aeroplanes visited the fields during the festivities including record-breakers Miss Winifred Spooner in her Puss Moth and Mr R.R. Bentley in his Sports Avian. The latter, along with Mr R.W.H. Knight flying a Monocoupe, whose sole claim to fame was a farcical ditching in the River Wye at Monmouth the previous year, landed at Splott Tidefields en route to Bridgend to view the progress being made by Mr Whitaker and his team.

Progress indeed seemed so well advanced that Capt. W.R. Bailey and Mr Charles H. Keen, a wealthy local businessman who was the assistant managing director of the family firm of Guest Keen & Baldwins Iron & Steel and a director of G.K.N. Ltd, announced their intention of forming a flying club to be based at Splott and entered into negotiations with the council regarding the construction of a hangar on the site. Apparently oblivious to the activities at Wenvoe they too chose the name Cardiff Flying Club until a letter of objection from Mr E.A. Brailey forced them to think again; the name Cardiff Aeroplane Club was chosen instead.

On Saturday 13 June a small presentation of aviation was given at Splott for the benefit of local councillors. Three aeroplanes arrived. D.H.80A Puss Moth G-ABBH flown from Heston by its owner, Mr H.A. Brock, and two D.H.60 Gipsy Moths from Bristol flown by Mr A.H. Downs-Shaw, chairman of the Bristol and Wessex Aeroplane Club, and Mr Norman Edgar, a Bristol aircraft dealer who was arguably to contribute more to the development of air transport in South Wales and the West County than any other person. Also present was Cllr Richard Ashley-Hall of Bristol. A businessman and private pilot, he had been a founder member of the Bristol & Wessex Aeroplane Club, was the chairman of the Bristol Airport Management Committee and a member of the Racing Committee of The Royal Aero Club. A knowledgeable and articulate advocate of aviation, Ashley-Hall was full of praise for the Cardiff site but made the prophetic remark: 'It will be even better provided the water is kept off the turf.' It must, of course, be remembered that all pre-war aerodromes, both civil and military, had grass surfaces, hard runways being unknown until the early years of the Second World War.

On the following Monday, Ashley-Hall addressed the Cardiff Rotary Club on the subject of aviation and such was the attendance that extra seats had to be brought into the hall. It could have done little to convince the doubtful, however, when news was received that one of Saturday's visitors, Mr H.A. Brock, along with his passenger, had died on Sunday in the blazing wreckage of his Puss Moth on a lonely road at Verneuil sur Avre, France, while en route from Heston to Le Mans, where they had intended to watch the closing stages of the twenty-four-hour motor race.

Barnard's Aerial Circus, the first true flying circus, visited Splott on Saturday and Sunday, 27 and 28 June in the course of a seven-month tour of the country. It visited 118 towns and cities in fifty counties, staged 370 performances before more than a million paying spectators and carried over 40,000 passengers.

The circus was led by Capt. C.D. Barnard, a pilot who had achieved considerable fame as a result of a number of long-distance record-breaking flights between 1928 and 1930 most of them at the controls of the fleet's flagship the Fokker F.VIIA G-EBTS *The Spider*. That interesting aeroplane, originally part of the fleet of the Dutch airline KLM, had been imported into the UK some years previously and under the name *Princess Xenia*, had been used by Capt. R.H. McIntosh on a number of unsuccessful long-distance record attempts. Re-engined with a 500hp Bristol Jupiter XI engine it had enjoyed more success in the hands of Barnard and his eccentric employer, the Duchess of Bedford, on return flights to India and South Africa. Reconfigured to accommodate fourteen passengers it now led a fleet consisting of a Spartan Three Seater, Desoutter, C.19MKIII Autogiro and the only Potez 36 ever to be based in Britain.

More aerial thrills were in store for the public when the Cardiff Flying Club staged an air pageant at Wenvoe on 1 August. In ideal weather conditions the proceedings commenced with joy riding which continued until the early afternoon when the Lord Mayor of Cardiff, Alderman R.G. Hill-Snook, made a stirring speech, cut a ribbon, and formally declared the pageant open. Soon afterwards sixteen light aeroplanes, many of them manufacturer's demonstration models, took to the air led by De Havilland test pilot Hugh Buckingham in D.H.80A Puss Moth, G-ABOF, with the Lord Mayor aboard, and flew in formation over the city for half an hour. The remainder of the afternoon was taken up with a flying display and two air races of eleven and thirty-three miles, both of which were won by Hugh Buckingham flying G-ABOF.

Meanwhile at Swansea Sands, South Wales Airways enjoyed a less successful afternoon when one of their Avros, G-AASS, became bogged down in a patch of soft sand where it remained until submerged by the rising tide and was subsequently written off.

An event of little significance in itself, but a portent of things to come, took place in the Cardiff Magistrates Court on 13 August when John Rogers, a demonstration pilot employed by the British agents of the German Klemm aircraft manufacturing company, appeared charged with failing to produce his pilot's licence when required to do so by a police officer. At that time it was a requirement that pilots carried their licence whenever they flew, a rule that was seldom observed and never enforced. Evidence was given that Rogers had landed at Splott on 15 June and when asked to produce his licence had stated that he had left it at home.

The Lord Mayor of Cardiff, Alderman R.G. Hill-Snook (in top hat), cutting the ribbon to declare the Cardiff Flying Club Air Pageant at Wenvoe Aerodrome open on 15 August 1931. The tall figure in flying overalls towards the left of the picture is Capt. Cecil Baker, the club's instructor who was killed later that year. The two aeroplanes are (from left to right): D.H.80A Puss Moth G-ABOF of the de Havilland Aircraft Co. and Avro Avian IVM G-ABIB Peri of British Petroleum. (Colin Butters)

The prosecution explained that the maximum penalty was a fine of £200 or six months imprisonment but the bench considered a fine of 30s to be sufficient. He was given fourteen days to pay.

Where the unfortunate Mr Rogers led, many others, included among them some well-known names, were to follow as, undeterred by the bench's lenient view, the Cardiff City Police Force continued to mount a relentless campaign against pilot licencing and aircraft documentation offences of even the most trivial nature until they became one of the most despised organisations in pre-war British civil aviation history.

Membership of the Cardiff Aeroplane Club was building up rapidly and on 22 September its first aeroplane, a D.H.60G Gipsy Moth G-ABRO, arrived at Splott piloted by Flg-Off. M.R. Edmondes, a director of the club. At about the same time Flg-Off. James Bunning was appointed as club instructor and, not to be outdone by the Cardiff Flying Club, an air pageant incorporating a London-Cardiff air race to be run under Royal Aero Club rules was organised for 3 October.

The pageant was an unprecedented success. To quote the magazine *Flight*, 'the meeting itself was, we hope, a foretaste of the way in which aviation matters will be handled in Cardiff in the future. It was excellently run with few flaws in the organisation.'

Some 25,000 members of the public paid over £1,200 admission money and no less than fifty-two aeroplanes of various types arrived. Guests at a private luncheon for club members, hosted by the Lord Mayor, included Sir Samuel Instone and Sir Arthur Whitten-Brown, the transatlantic pioneer.

The flying programme commenced with joy riding which was halted a little after 2.30 p.m. in anticipation of the arrival of the competitors in the London-Cardiff race. The race was a handicap event with the fourteen competitors being flagged away from Heston Aerodrome, about a mile north of the present Heathrow Airport, in inverse order of speed to route via a turning point at Beachley to Cardiff. Two of them, H.C. Mayers (Comper Swift) and C. Amherst Villiers (Martinsyde A.V.1) dropped out en route, the rest of the field being led across the finishing line by Flg-Off. H.R.A. Edwards in his diminutive Avro Baby, G-EAUM, having achieved an average speed of 81.5mph.

A varied programme of events followed including aerobatics by such diverse types as Comper Swift, Moth and a Bristol Bulldog fighter flown by the Bristol Aeroplane Co. test pilot, C.F. Uwins. Another well-known test pilot, A.H. Rawson, demonstrated a Ciereva C.19 Autogiro. Crazy flying and flour bombing competitions followed before a two-lap short circuit air race between Cardiff and Newport which was won by Miss Winifred Brown in her Sports Avian, G-ABED. The programme concluded with a flypast of fifteen aircraft and a parachute descent by Capt. E.W. Stewart.

As the year drew to its end Cardiff flying enthusiasts looked back on what appeared to have been a year of remarkable achievement. With two active aerodromes and two flying clubs established and plans well advanced for a demonstration passenger service between Splott and Bristol (Whitchurch) aerodromes sponsored by the *Bristol Evening Times and Echo* using an Avro Ten airliner leased from Imperial Airways, further exciting progress in the coming year seemed assured. Then two severe blows struck in quick succession.

Heavy winter rainfall revealed the inadequacy of the drainage work carried out at Splott. By mid-November the aerodrome was totally waterlogged and all flying activity was forced to cease. An Air Ministry inspection carried out for the purpose of granting a permanent licence to the aerodrome resulted in failure, an Air Ministry spokesman stating that: 'In the interest of aviation a certificate has not been granted to Cardiff Aerodrome.'

At Wenvoe worse was to come. On the afternoon of Sunday 13 December Capt. Cecil Baker, the club instructor, decided to conclude a flying lesson in the Avian G-EBYO with an impromptu aerobatic display above the aerodrome. After a series of loops and rolls the aeroplane entered a spin at about 2,500ft from which it did not recover and struck the ground in the centre of the aereodrome in a steep nose-down attitude. Baker in the front seat was killed instantly but his pupil Mr H.O. Evans, a Fairwater building contractor, when cut from the wreckage was found to have escaped with relatively minor injuries.

The accident proved to be the death knell of the Cardiff Flying Club which ceased operations never to restart, although the aerodrome continued to be used on an occasional basis by visiting aeroplanes until it came under new management some years later.

Quite suddenly all the effort put in by so many people seemed to have been in vain and the future looked very bleak indeed.

13
The Phoenix Rises

As the new year dawned, Cardiff city fathers found themselves on the horns of a dilemma having spent some £19,000 on the production of a white elephant of considerable proportions. Eventually, after much soul searching, they decided to attempt to avert an embarrassing political fiasco by voting an additional £6,000 to finance further drainage work. George Whitaker and his team worked throughout the following months and, although the outcome was never entirely satisfactory, the surface still being prone to waterlogging in extremely wet weather, by and large the gamble paid off and an area measuring 600 yards by 400 yards finally received an Air Ministry licence on 14 April 1932. Further work to reclaim more of the surface and to construct a hangar continued throughout the summer months.

Club flying recommenced immediately and on 20 April the aerodrome played host to the year's first visitor, the well-known flier Pt-Off. John Grierson RAF at the controls of his D.H.60G Gipsy Moth, G-AAJP, *Rouge et Noir*, in which he had flown from Karachi to Lympne in four days ten hours and thirty minutes the previous year.

Undoubtedly relieved at having survived the previous winter's débâcle without too much egg on their faces, Cardiff City Council gave great prominence to their aerodrome facility during Cardiff Civic Week which commenced on 1 June 1932. It was in newspaper advertisements publicising the week's aerial events that the aerodrome was first referred to as Pengam Aerodrome after the district to the north of the boundary, and soon the original name of Splott, which has always caused a combination of disbelief and mirth among strangers to the locality, fell into disuse. Later still, the aerodrome came to be known as Pengam Moors.

The principal aerial event of the week was the arrival at Pengam of Sir Alan Cobham's National Aviation Day Display fleet on 1 June, its first visit to South Wales. Sir Alan was greeted on his arrival by the Lord Mayor, Alderman C.W. Melhuish and other civic dignitaries while the traditional aerial parade over the city by nine aircraft of the circus fleet took place. The fleet consisted of Airspeed A.S.4 Ferry, G-ABSI, *Youth of Britain II*, a three-engined ten-seater cabin biplane custom-built by the emergent Airspeed company to Sir Alan's specification for a joy riding machine; H.P.W10 airliner, G-EBMR, *City of Pretoria*, piloted by Capt. E.B. Fielden of Aviation Tours Ltd.; Gipsy Moth; Tiger Moth; Southern Martlet; Blackburn Bluebird; Desoutter; Cierva C.19 MK IV autogiro; B.A.C. VII glider; Comper Swift, radio equipped to enable its pilot to execute aerobatic manoeuvres at the request of members of the public; and the inevitable Avro 504K. The cost of passenger flights varied from £1 in the *City of Pretoria* to 5s in the glider, except for the lucky winners of the *Western Mail* essay competition on the subject of 'Why I want to fly'. The reason given by the winners, whose ages ranged from thirteen to eighty-seven, were many and varied, one, a Merthyr miner, stating that he was bored stiff and ready to die whilst another, the late Mr Norman Jones of Llandaff, confessed to the author, some sixty years after the event, that he achieved success by submitting multiple entries. It was during the visit that the Airspeed Ferry

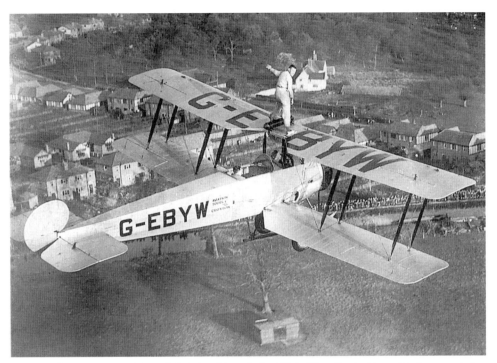

Wing-walking on Avro 504K of Aviation Tours Ltd, 1931. The pilot is Capt. H. Lawson. It has proved impossible to positively identify the wing-walker as Pat O'Hara. (Aerofilms Ltd)

made a return flight to Bristol (Whitchurch) Aerodrome which led Sir Alan to claim to have been responsible for the first public transport passenger flights across the Bristol Channel.

Having performed in Cardiff on 1 and 2 June the fleet moved on to Lock's Common, Porthcawl, where they gave a performance on 3 June. Later in the year, on 28 August, they also appeared at Park Mill, Gower. Flying from a field to the west of Vennaway Lane at its junction with the A4118.

No sooner had one flying circus left Pengam than another arrived in the form of 'The Crimson Fleet', operated by Modern Airways Ltd, under the direction of one M.A. Ap Rhys-Pryce. The fleet consisted of three aeroplanes, an Avro 504K piloted by E.M. Slade, a Gipsy Moth piloted by C.R. Cubitt and a Spartan Three Seater operated by the all-female crew of Pauline Gower, pilot and Dorothy Spicer, engineer. They remained at Pengam from 3 to 11 June giving a display every evening and apparently flying from Lock's Common during the day.

The fleet's size was temporarily diminished during the Cardiff evening display of 8 June when the Gipsy Moth, which was taking part in a stunt in which a supposed felon fleeing from pursuing police officers ran from the crowd and made off in it, was struck amidships by the Spartan which was departing on a joy ride – to the severe detriment of both aeroplanes. Happily Cubitt, who was concealed in the Moth's cockpit, and the 'thief', who was half in and half out of the moving aircraft, were unhurt and Pauline Gower and her two passengers when released from the wreckage were found to have suffered only superficial injuries. The affair proved to be another aviation first for Cardiff having its next installment in the King's Bench Division before an amused Mr Justice Acton in October 1933, when the action of Cubitt and another *v.* Gower, brought under Section 9 (i) of the Air Navigation Act 1920, became the first lawsuit in the UK, and possibly the world, arising from a ground collision between two aircraft. Miss Gower was held to be at fault and Cubitt and his partner were awarded £222 damages.

Replacement aeroplanes were soon acquired, however, and the tour resumed without interruption. It only remained for Ap Rhys-Pryce to present the Lord Mayor with a new bowler hat to replace one that had blown away during a complimentary joy ride, before the circus departed for Lock's Common where they appeared to have spent most of the rest of the summer. Various news items describe a charter flight carried out by Cubitt from Lock's Common to Norwich and back on 28 June when he landed back at Porthcawl with the aid of car headlights at 10.40 p.m., a successful precautionary landing by E.M. Slade and his passenger H.S. Gomes, the circus wing-walker, in a field near the Old Post, Bonvilston, on 4 August and the Crimson Fleets participation in the Porthcawl Carnival celebrations on 20 August.

The RAF was also in evidence during Civic Week with a flypast over the city of five Bristol Bulldog fighters of 32 Squadron on 6 June and a visit by the Westland Wapitis of 501 Squadron led by Sqn Ldr Sugden on 11 June. After leaving Pengam for their base at Filton the Wapitis also treated Cardiffians to a formation flypast over the city.

On Monday 11 July the long-awaited scheduled air service trial between Cardiff and Bristol (Whitchurch) Aerodromes commenced, the object being to ascertain demand. The operation which was planned for one week only, was mounted by The British Air Navigation Co., trading as the Bristol-Cardiff Air Navigation Co. using that well-known aeroplane Fokker F.VIIA, G-EBTS, under the command of its equally well-known pilot Capt. C.D. Barnard.

Fokker FVIIA — The Spider — was the flagship of Barnard's Aerial Circus in 1931 and operated the experimental Cardiff-Bristol air service in July 1932. (Kenneth G. Wakefield)

Sir Alan Cobham (in flying overalls) and local dignitaries standing in front of Handley Page W10 Airliner at the National Aviation Day display at Lock's Common, Porthcawl, 3 June 1932. (Porthcawl Museum)

Four daily return services were scheduled with coach connections between the aerodromes and the Angel Hotel, Cardiff and the Grand Hotel, Bristol, respectively. The scheduled time between hotels was forty minutes, about half that of the scheduled railway journey and the fares were set competitively at 15s single and £1 7s 6d return. Once again the air-minded *Western Mail* ran an essay competition for free tickets on the service, the subject being, 'My vision of Cardiff as an airport in 1942'. Needless to say unforeseen future events rendered even the most imaginative predictions well wide of the mark.

As so often seems to be the case on such occasions, a spell of fine weather that had lasted for weeks broke, and throughout the trial Barnard had to cope with rain, low cloud and thunderstorms, over an inch of rain fell on Cardiff on the Wednesday alone, but nevertheless all flights were completed on schedule with two extra return journeys fitted in on the Saturday. In all, 199 fare-paying passengers, mostly businessmen, were carried along with various civic dignitaries, complimentary ticket holders and the winners of the *Western Mail* competition, proving beyond doubt the potential for a permanent scheduled operation on the route.

The challenge was taken up by Norman Edgar of Bristol who inaugurated an air ferry service linking the two cities on 26 September 1932 using a D.H.83 Fox Moth, G-ABYO, a single-engine biplane capable of carrying three passengers in an enclosed cabin ahead of the pilot's open cockpit. The ferry operated two return services per day leaving Bristol at 10.45 a.m. and 2.45 p.m. and Cardiff at 11.15 a.m. and 3.15 p.m. The fares for the twenty-minute flight were set at 12s 6d single and £1 2s 6d return. Passengers could be conveyed to and from Cardiff city centre by Pidgeon's Hire Service, who also acted as agents for Norman Edgar, for 1s.

Sir Alan Cobham's National Aviation Day display in 1932. Aircraft from left to right are Avro 504K G-ABHI of the Cornwall Aviation Co. and Airspeed A.S.4 Ferry G-ABSJ. The location is uncertain. (Stan Reynolds)

Airspeed A.S.4 Ferry of the National Aviation Day display in 1932. (Stan Reynolds)

Cierva C.19 of the National Aviation Day display in 1932. (Stan Reynolds)

City centre transport at Bristol was free. The service proved to be an immediate success.

On 1 October Norman Edgar undertook a more ambitious venture, the transportation of an entire rugby team plus officials across the Bristol Channel. Although his own company did not have the capacity to mount such an operation he took advantage of the fact that the Bristol and Wessex Aeroplane Club were holding their annual garden party and persuaded various club members and visiting pilots to co-operate.

And so it came to pass that seventeen members of Clifton Rugby Club were flown in a small armada of light aeroplanes through low cloud and turbulence to keep a fixture with a Glamorgan Wanderers XV. After a drawn game the team flew back to Bristol and were able to claim to be the first rugby team to have travelled by air to keep an official fixture in the UK.

On 15 October the Cardiff Aeroplane Club held an at home day to coincide with the running of the London-Cardiff air race. The event was principally a private function for members and their guests although 4,000 members of the public paid sixpence each to view the proceedings from the public enclosure. A large number of light aeroplanes arrived from various parts of the country and the newly completed hangar was filled to capacity, the temporary one being converted to a comfortable club house for the occasion.

The race, run over the same course as the previous year, attracted nine entrants and was won in gusty conditions by M.D.L. Scott of Eastern Air Transport Ltd, flying Puss Moth G-ABOF, the aircraft that had been so successful in the previous year's Wenvoe races.

There followed an aerobatic competition won by Flt-Lt Christopher Clarkson in a Comper Swift and a spot landing competition won by Capt. E.W. Percival in a Percival Gull. A hidden treasure competition in which the winner was the pilot who touched down nearest to the treasure, a gold propelling pencil buried in the turf, had a less successful outcome. After the winner had been declared, the club engineer, Mr G.E. Watkiss, who had buried the pencil, set out to retrieve it. Despite much scratching and digging by Watkiss and others, the earth failed to give up its secret and for all I know the pencil is there to this day.

Norman Edgar assisting Mrs Fraser and her daughter – the first two passengers to use the Bristol-Cardiff ferry – into D.H.83 Fox Moth G-ABYO. In the cockpit is Flg-Off. W.N.L. Cope, who later became a familiar figure in Cardiff as the instructor of the Cardiff Aeroplane Club. (Kenneth G. Wakefield)

A further gloom was cast over the proceedings by the arrival of members of the Cardiff City Police resulting in three visiting pilots being prosecuted for failing to produce their licences. Public joy riding by a Fox Moth and Puss Moth of Norman Edgar brought the proceedings to a close.

As winter drew on, all eyes were on the state of the aerodrome surface which to everybody's relief withstood the rain, allowing both the Cardiff Aeroplane Club and the Cardiff-Bristol ferry to operate unhindered until the following spring.

Now is an appropriate time in this story to pause for reflection. The events just described took place only twenty-nine years after the Wright brothers first powered flight at Kitty Hawk and less than twenty-two years after Ernest Sutton's first tentative hops at Oxwich. During those years, great strides had been made in aviation technology worldwide, spurred on to a great extent by the events of the First World War. The world speed record stood at 406mph, the altitude record at over 43,000ft, while the world flight refuelled endurance records were approaching a month. Both poles had been overflown, oceans and continents crossed and Mount Everest was about to be viewed from above for the first time.

Locally Cardiff had an aerodrome, albeit with only a part of its surface licensed but nevertheless sufficient to support the activities of an emergent flying club and the beginnings of a scheduled air transport operation. Developments in those early years, however, were as nothing when compared to the progress made in the following seven. Not only did the advance of technology continue to accelerate, but aviation activities began to proliferate rapidly. They also began to diversify into quite distinct and separate branches.

Up to this point it has been logical to chronicle events in the order in which they occurred. From 1933 onwards, however, it seems more appropriate to examine the following seven years developments under separate headings while at the same time paying as much attention to chronology as possible.

D.H.80A Puss Moth of Norman Edgar, which was occasionally used on the Bristol-Cardiff ferry. (Kenneth G. Wakefield)

D.H.83 Fox Moth G-ABYO of Norman Edgar inaugurated the Bristol-Cardiff ferry service on 26 September 1932. (Kenneth G. Wakefield)

14
Sporting Aviation

With Pengam Aerodrome finally established as a viable proposition, Cardiff City Council gave thought to its day-to-day management and as a result entered into an agreement with the Cardiff Aeroplane Club. Under the terms of the agreement effective from 13 March 1933, the Lord Mayor, his deputy and five members of the council joined the club committee which in effect doubled as the aerodrome management committee. The club undertook to oversee the running of the aerodrome, collect landing fees and take on a four-year lease at £10 per annum of a clubhouse to be erected by the council. The council for their part agreed to provide labour to maintain, improve and extend the aerodrome surface. The outcome in effect was that the club's full time staff of two, its instructor and engineer, also became the aerodrome's full time staff of two!

From 1 April the Cardiff Aeroplane Club was admitted to the Government subsidy scheme under which it received £25 for each new pilot trained and £10 for any A or B licence renewed or any pre-1921 RAF pilot to qualify for a licence. The club was still very much in its infancy, numbering among its membership only five licensed pilots, but with twenty-five student pilots under training the newly appointed instructor, Flg-Off. W.N.L. Cope, was finding the single Gipsy Moth barely equal to the task.

The club played host to an unexpected guest on 16 May 1933 when the Prince of Wales, who had arrived at Pengam earlier in the day aboard his newly acquired Vickers Viastra, G-ACCC, to fulfill an engagement in the city, returned to discover that the aeroplane had not yet returned from a flight to Bristol. The Prince and his equerry, by then afforded the luxury of travelling in lounge suits and bowler hats instead of the flying suits and helmets of earlier years, spent their fifteen-minute wait inspecting the club premises and chatting to members. It was presumably as a result of the club's hospitality that the Prince consented to become its patron in June 1933.

The following month the club extended its hospitality to two other well-known personalities, Jim Mollison and his wife Amy, formerly Miss Amy Johnson. The Mollisons were at that time engaged on a long-distance record breaking attempt using a modified D.H.84 Dragon I, G-ACCV, *Seafarer*, in which they had originally planned to fly from London to New York, prior to attempting a non-stop flight from New York to Baghdad. The project was fated from the very beginning. Their first attempt, from Croydon, on 8 June 1933 had been frustrated prior to take off when the Dragon's undercarriage collapsed under the weight of the 603 gallons of fuel, contained mainly in a large tank which occupied most of the aeroplane's cabin.

After repairs, the Mollisons decided that the seven-mile-long natural runway at Pendine Sands, Carmarthenshire, the scene of several World Land Speed Record attempts provided a safer option and with that end in view *Seafarer* was positioned to Pengam on 3 July. There she embarked two De Havilland employees prior to departing for Pendine. Fate, however, still failed to smile on the two adventurers and, after an unsuccessful wait for favourable

Jim and Amy Mollison with Seafarer,
7 July 1933. (Associated Press)

weather conditions coupled with good moonlight, *Seafarer* was defuelled to 100 gallons and positioned back to Pengam on 7 July.

The all-black biplane was put on public exhibition in the club hangar and between then and 15 July, when Jim Mollison flew her back to the De Havilland Aerodrome at Stag Lane, many thousands of Cardiffians paid 6*d* each to view her. During their stay Jim and Amy were entertained by members of the Cardiff Aeroplane Club and attended various local social and public functions.

Subsequently *Seafarer* was positioned directly from Stag Lane to Pendine on 22 July and left for New York later that day. Thirty-nine hours later in the course of an attempted downwind landing at night at Bridgeport, Connecticut, by an exhausted Jim Mollison, *Seafarer* overturned and was wrecked, her crew being fortunate to escape with relatively minor injuries.

Perfect weather attended the Cardiff Aeroplane Club's air pageant which coincided with the running of the annual London-Cardiff Air Race on 22 July 1933 when some 25,000 spectators and fifty-five visiting aircraft attended.

Pilots visiting the event would have done well to have heeded the advice of C.G. Grey, the irascible editor of the magazine *The Aeroplane*, whose assistant editor had been one of the victims of the Cardiff City Police's document purge the previous year:

> *…to profit from previous experience and carry licences, log books, certificates of airworthiness, certificates of registration, health certificates, birth certificates, marriage licences, dog licences, wireless licences, volumes, brochures, passports and all matters remotely bearing on the International Convention for Air Navigation to the last futile and infuriating detail.*

D.H.84 Dragon I Seafarer, *piloted by J.A. Mollison, approaching Cardiff, 7 July 1933.* (Associated Press)

The pageant was declared open by Sir Phillip Sassoon, Under Secretary of State for Air, who arrived from Hendon aboard a RAF Hawker Hart. Thereafter the public witnessed a flying display including aerobatics by Capt. Cyril Uwins in a Bristol Bulldog, a formation display by the Westland Wallaces of 501 Squadron, crazy flying by H.B. Field in an Avro and two parachute descents – one by B.G. de Greeuw, using a Russell Lobe parachute, and the other, the first free fall descent seen in Wales, by 'Wingy' Wyndham. Wyndham was a well-known one-armed Hollywood stuntman of the time, whose descent terminated among the spectators, fortunately without injury to anybody.

The London-Cardiff race provided spectators with a thrilling finish. A.J. Styran, at the controls of Sir Derwent Hall-Caine's Leopard Moth, G-ACHC, crossed the finishing line only seconds ahead of Alex Henshaw's Comper Swift, G-ACGL, and Norman Edgar's Puss Moth entered by Richard Cadman of Cardiff Aeroplane Club with *Western Mail* reporter J.C. Griffith-Jones aboard. Edgar Percival flying Percival Gull, G-ACHA, the fourth pilot to cross the line, won the Norman Nash Cup for the fastest time (149.5mph).

Sadly, it was to be the popular Styran's last win in British air racing for he was to be killed in a flying accident at Hawkhurst, Kent, on 1 October 1933.

Public joy riding to a late hour brought a most successful day to its conclusion.

In July 1933 the Cardiff Aeroplane Club, in conjunction with the *Western Mail*, launched the *Western Mail* Flying Scholarship Scheme, a novel innovation which both captured the public imagination and provided the club with a welcome source of revenue.

For an entry fee of £1, candidates entered a selection process consisting of a half hour trial flight, the best six going forward to a second trial from which the two winning candidates were selected. The winners received a year's free club membership and free tuition leading to the grant of an A licence. The scheme proved to be an outstanding success attracting some 450 entries of which about seventy-five per cent eventually flew. Selection commenced on 5 August when a second Gipsy Moth, G-ACJG, was acquired and the aid of Flg-Off. J.E. Jurdon, a serving RAF flying instructor on home leave, was enlisted to cope with demand, and continued until November. The eventual winners were Messrs C.H. Mogg, a twenty-seven-year-old Penarth insurance inspector and H.R. Griffiths a thirty-one-year-old Newport solicitor.

A move to its new premises by the end of the year symbolised the end of the club's formative period and heralded what promised to be an assured future.

On 3 March 1934 Cardiff Aeroplane Club member, Mr W.G. Nicol, a Kenyan resident, took delivery of a new B.K. Swallow, powered by a Salmson A.D.9 radial engine in which he and his wife proposed to return to Kenya. The British Klemm Aeroplane Co., who built the aeroplane under licence from a German design, took advantage of the occasion to demonstrate a similar model, powered by a British Pobjoy engine to club members, eight of whom availed themselves of the opportunity to fly it. Although no further sales resulted at the time, a developed version, the B.A. Swallow, one of the safest light aeroplanes ever built, was to become a familiar sight at Pengam in years to come.

The following week on Sunday 11 March the forerunner of another famous marque of light aereoplanes, a Miles M.2 Hawk low wing two-seat monoplane, was also put through its paces for the benefit of club members.

A curious anomaly in the law up to that time was that, although the minimum age for the issue of an A licence allowing a pilot to carry passengers was seventeen, there was no stipulated minimum age at which a student pilot could fly solo, a fact taken advantage of by several young people including Charles Cadman, son of Mr Richard Cadman, a director of Cardiff Aeroplane Club, who during his Easter holidays from Shrewsbury School, was sent on his first solo flight by Flg-Off. Cope on 26 April 1934 at the age of fifteen. Young Charles' achievement was not a record, that distinction belonging to one Ovid Victor Ottley who had made his first solo flight at Abridge, Essex, on 8 April 1934, aged fourteen. Unfortunately, however, the death of another youthful soloist in Yorkshire in July 1934 resulted in the prohibition of solo flying by those under seventeen compelling Charles Cadman to wait another two years before repeating the experience.

The Cardiff Aeroplane Club found themselves faced with competition from 25 June 1934 when Robert Thomas of South Wales Airways took over the lease of Wenvoe Aerodrome where he opened a flying school equipped with a single Gipsy Moth.

It was Thomas' long term aim to secure a Government contract to establish an Elementary and Reserve Flying School on the site. Such organisations, operated by civilian contractors, provided elementary flying training to pilots of the RAF and RAF Reserve. Although his endeavours in that direction came to nought, there can be little doubt that his tireless lobbying of the authorities did have the effect of convincing the Air Ministry that the Vale of Glamorgan was an eminently suitable venue for military aviation activities.

The club and the Deputy Lord Mayor played host to the crews of twelve Westland Wallaces of 501 Squadron led by their CO, Sqn Ldr W. Elliott DFC, on Monday 16 July. Also at that time, because one of the Moths was out of service for its certificate of airworthiness inspection, a D.H.82 Tiger Moth, the first of many to be used by the club, was leased to replace it.

In August Flg-Off. J.D. Rose, who was standing in for Flg-Off Cope during his annual leave, introduced several members to night flying aided by flares on the landing area and a full moon but it was decided to abandon the idea until more suitable aerodrome lighting became available.

In contrast to the previous year, the weather for the London-Cardiff air race and flying display held on 6 October 1934 was far from good causing the display to be abandoned. Of the few visiting aeroplanes the most imposing was the Handley Page H.P.42E *Heracles* of Imperial Airways, the largest aeroplane to land at Pengam up to that time, which was used for joy riding. Her crew consisted of the once-familiar figure at Pengam, Capt. Fred Dismore, and First Officer J.W.G. James, a recently appointed young co-pilot who in post-war years was to become the highly respected Director of Flight Operations of British European Airways.

Despite the weather the London-Cardiff race was run. First away was Mr W.T.S. 'Sam' Lewis, a director of Cardiff Aeroplane Club and Honorary Airport Manager of Pengam, piloting one of the club's Moths, the scratch man being Sir Charles Rose in his Miles Hawk Major. Of the fifteen starters three retired en route, presumably due to the weather conditions.

First across the line was Lord Patrick Crichton-Stuart's Hendy Hobo, G-AAIG, a diminutive low wing monoplane powered by a 90hp Pobjoy Cataract engine flown by Flt Lt R. Duncanson, ahead of A.H. Cook (Comper Swift) and L. Lipton (Gipsy Moth).

An incident-packed few minutes followed as the competitors landed at Pengam. First the winning Hobo, which had completed its landing run, was struck amidships by Owen Cathcart-Jones' British Klemm Eagle which had not. Hardly had the dust settled before Sir Charles Rose, the fourth man home, apparently suffered a power loss on final approach. The Hawk Major failed to make it to the landing area and came to rest on the boundary hedge. Fortunately, nobody was hurt, and, although badly damaged, all three aeroplanes eventually flew again.

With the installation of G.E.C. shadow bar lighting in March 1935 the Cardiff Aeroplane Club commenced night flying training in earnest and also earned additional revenue by offering nocturnal joy rides to the general public.

Following the success of the first *Western Mail* Flying Scholarship Scheme it was decided to run a second one in 1935. Announced in March with the entry fee reduced to 10*s* it attracted 600 applicants necessitating the employment of a second instructor, Flg-Off. R.C. Parker and the acquisition of a third Gipsy Moth, G-ABOA, formerly the private aeroplane of Mr S.K. Davies, who had disposed of it favour of Miles M.2P Hawk Major, G-ADDK, *y Ddraig Goch*.

Selection began in April and was not completed until the following January, the winners being: Miss Diana Fitchett, a Newport teacher; Capt. G.W. Jones, also of Newport; an insurance manager; and two Cardiff men, Mr Peter Farr, a student, and Mr R.T. Gifkins, an electrician.

An aerobatic display by Flg-Off. Cope at Roath Park on the occasion of the Taff Swim held on 20 July inaugurated a tradition that continued until the war. Club aeroplanes, either singly or in formation also entertained crowds at various other outdoor events during the remainder of the 1930s.

Cardiff featured prominently in the British air racing calendar in September 1935 not only as the finishing point for the London-Cardiff race but, for the first time, as a staging point in the King's Cup Air Race as well.

The King's Cup event which took place over two days, 6 and 7 September, consisted of a 953-mile round Britain race, starting and finishing at Hatfield, Hertfordshire, with landings at Glasgow, Newtownards, Manchester and Cardiff. The twenty-nine entrants were divided into two classes for aircraft of under and over 150hp. The first ten in each class then went forward to the final, seven laps of a fifty-mile closed circuit again starting and finishing at Hatfield run on the second day. Both Cardiff Corporation and the *Western Mail* supported the event by donating prizes, for the fastest time to Cardiff in the over 150hp and under 150hp classes respectively.

The first competitor, Capt. E.W. Percival flying Percival Mew Gull, G-ACND, and attired as always in lounge suit and trilby hat arrived at Pengam at 12.59 p.m, winning the Cardiff Corporation prize. He was followed at 1.07 p.m. by another designer/pilot, F.G. Miles flying Miles M.5 Sparrowhawk, G-ADNL, who won the *Western Mail* prize. The remaining competitors arrived and departed Pengam until about 4.00 p.m. For the record the event was won by Flt Lt Tommy Rose flying Miles M.3B Falcon Six, G-ADLC.

Due to the fact that Sir Alan Cobham's National Aviation Day Display visited Pengam on 25 September it was decided not to hold the traditional air pageant to coincide with the London-Cardiff race held on 21 September but to follow the main event with a short circuit pylon race instead.

On the day the weather was atrocious with thunderstorms, heavy rain, poor visibility and a bitterly cold wind. The start was delayed until 4.00 p.m. when the first competitor, D.M. Bey, flying a B.A. Swallow was flagged away. The handicappers obviously did a first class job – the first aeroplane to appear at Cardiff being B.K. Eagle 2, G-ACRG, flown by Flt Lt J.B. Wilson, but even as the crowd were cheering him to the finishing line, over the sea wall appeared Capt. Edgar Percival's Mew Gull, G-ACND, to pip Wilson to the post by just three seconds, having averaged 218mph over the 120-mile course. All competitors finished within the space of three minutes. Due to the lateness of the hour the pylon race was abandoned.

At the end of the year Cardiff Aeroplane Club disposed of Gipsy Moth G-ABOA and also bade farewell to Flg-Off. Cope who left to take up an instructional post with the newly formed RAF Reserve Flying School at Yatesbury. Flg-Off. Parker had also departed to commence a distinguished career with Imperial Airways and its successor B.O.A.C. As an interim measure C.R. Cubitt, by then chief pilot of Western Airways, acted as club instructor on a part-time basis until a suitable replacement could be found.

The successor arrived in March 1936 in the form of Mr G.M.S. Kemp, a former RAF sergeant pilot who since leaving the service in 1928 had been employed as an instructor at Newcastle and Birmingham and who, with the exception of wartime service, was to remain with the club and its successor the Glamorgan Flying Club at Rhoose for over thirty years.

One of George Kemp's first tasks was to ferry a Percival Gull Six, reportedly purchased by Charles Keen, from Reading to Cardiff on 16 March. The history of that aeroplane around that time is a little obscure. It appears never to have been used by the club but ultimately became the property of Mr S.K. Davies in May 1937.

Inclement weather in eastern England over the weekend of 19 and 20 September 1936 severely disrupted that year's London-Cardiff race and later was indirectly responsible for a tragic accident at Cardiff.

Owing to the weather a number of competitors including Edgar Percival in the well-fancied Mew Gull were unable to reach Heston in time for the start, resulting in a much depleted field.

The race was won by De Havilland test pilot R.J. Waight flying the one-off T.K.2 G-ADNO, a racing aeroplane designed and built by De Havilland apprentices, at an average speed of 189.72mph. Second was C.S. Napier at the controls of Percival Gull G-ADOE with L.J.C. Mitchell third in a D.H. Puss Moth.

About fifty visiting aircraft attending the meeting and 7,000 spectators witnessed a display which featured a parachute descent by Aberystwyth parachutist Gwyn Johns.

Several pilots put their aircraft through their paces that evening including Mr H.R. Dimock of the Ely Aero Club, Cambridgeshire, who in the words of the magazine *Flight*, 'put up one of the best ground and air demonstrations of the Drone that we have ever seen'. The Kronfeld Super Drone was a motorised glider whose engine, a 23hp Douglas Sprite was mounted on a pylon above and behind the pilot. Apparently the unfortunate Dimock's hat blew off and struck the propeller causing the Drone to crash into allotments adjoining the airport. Dimock was thrown clear sustaining only a cut above his eye but, concluded *Flight*, 'very little of the machine was left.'

The thin divide between comedy and tragedy was amply demonstrated the following day. The weather in much of England was such that many pilots were prevented from returning home on the Sunday and one of them, Mr Maurice E. King, a twenty-three-year-old director of the Norfolk and Norwich Aero Club, decided to pass the time with some local flying from Pengam in his B.A. Eagle, G-ADPN. Two Cardiff Aeroplane Club members, Messrs H.B. Elwell and T.J. Borg, accompanied him on the flight.

The Eagle was subsequently seen flying low in the vicinity of Mr Elwell's home in Wenallt Road, Rhiwbina, with Elwell waving to his wife from one of the back seats. It then made a very low pass across Whitchurch Golf Course and at near rooftop height followed Wenallt Road in a northerly direction towards the Elwell residence which was a considerable distance along the road which has a fairly steep uphill gradient. It seems that King underestimated the gradient and failed to give due consideration to the high ground to the north. Having passed the house, probably with a decreasing airspeed due to the climb he was seen to execute a steeply banked climbing turn away from the high ground, a manoeuvre that would have greatly increased the aeroplane's stalling speed. The Eagle stalled and spun from low level into a field adjoining the road where it burst into flames killing all three occupants instantly.

The following Thursday George Kemp and Wattie Watkiss had the sombre and in the author's experience, messy, task of scattering Harold Elwell's ashes over the Wenallt from a Club aeroplane.

Life, as it always does, went on. In October S.K. Davies' Hawk Major, G-ADDK, became the property of the Cardiff Aeroplane Club to be joined in the hangar the following month by B.A. Swallow 2 (Cirrus Minor engine) the property of Capt. C.D. Godfrey who was learning to fly with the club at the age of sixty-nine. It is probable that Civilian Coupe G-ABNT, operated by Mr G.O. Rees of Carmarthen from 1933 onwards, also spent at least some of its life as a Pengam resident before being put into store in Mr Rees' garage at the outbreak of war. It was resurrected many years later and is still airworthy at the time of writing.

As Christmas approached and children sang 'Hark! the herald-angels sing, Mrs Simpson's pinched our king', a nation that had been ruled by three monarchs in the space of 326 days looked forward to 1937 as Coronation Year despite increasing evidence that all was not well on the international stage.

It was the latter fact that caused the greatest disruption to civil aviation at Pengam during the years 1937 and 1938 when the formation of No.614 Squadron Auxiliary Air Force led to a great deal of building work and overall reorganisation, including the expansion of the airport to the north and west onto land previously used as allotments and moving the civil aviation entrance from Whitaker Road to Tweedsmuir Road.

The Coronation too, gave rise to much activity. On the day itself, 12 May 1937, long before television had spread to nearly every home in the land, aeroplanes were used to convey newspaper photographs and ciné film to all parts of the country. The *Western Mail*, for instance, received its first photographs at 2.00 p.m. Ciné film flown into Pengam by other operators was shown in Llanelli at 8.00 p.m. thanks to the efforts of George Kemp and S.K. Davies who carried it on to Jersey Marine Aerodrome in club aeroplanes.

Among Cardiff's Coronation celebrations was the Cardiff Coronation Air Rally held on Saturday 15 May when 15,000 spectators saw fifty-two light aeroplanes arrive at Pengam Moors. A somewhat ironic attraction was joy riding in the luxuriously appointed D.H.89 Dragon Rapide G-ADDD, which until recently had been the personal transport of the abdicated and exiled King Edward VIII but had then been acquired by Western Airways for use as a conventional airliner.

It would have been logical to have run the London-Cardiff race to coincide with the rally but in the event it was run on 10 July. In the face of a strong headwind and gusty conditions Geoffrey de Havilland junior flying the previous year's winning aeroplane, the T.K.2 G-ADNO, finished 100 yards in front of Alex Henshaw's Mew Gull, G-AEXF. J.C.V.K. Watson flying Miles Falcon Six G-ADLC was third.

On 8 August Mr S.K. Davies, who travelled extensively on the Continent in his private aeroplanes, suffered a forced landing near Dijon while en route from Cannes to Cardiff. The Gull suffered some damage but Mr Davies was unhurt.

Cardiff was again a staging point in the 1937 King's Cup Air Race which as previously was a two-day event starting and finishing at Hatfield. On the first day competitors flew in stages via Newcastle, Aberdeen, Glasgow and Newtownards to Dublin. On day two Saturday 11 September they retraced their route to Newtownards routing thereafter via Blackpool and Cardiff to Hatfield.

The race was marred by a bizarre accident on the first day when Miles M.3A Falcon Major G-AENG crashed at a turning point near Scarborough after encountering turbulence of such severity that its pilot, Wg Cdr E.G. Hilton, was thrown through the windscreen into the propeller leaving his navigator, Wg Cdr Percy Sherren, who was not a pilot, to crash to his death with the aeroplane.

Only thirteen of the twenty-seven starters reached Cardiff, led by a quite remarkable character – sixty-three-year-old Brigadier-General A.C. Lewin CBE, CMG, DSO, ADC, at the controls of his red Miles Whitney Straight, G-AEZO. Interviewed before the event he had stated, 'I have no great opinion of the value of air racing today. As a sport it is far behind, say, pig sticking, steeple chasing or polo, at least for the private owner and amateur… Personally I have entered on this one and only occasion merely for the sake of the experience it is offering me.'

The race was won by Charles E. Gardner flying Mew Gull G-AEKL, closely followed by the gallant Brigadier-General, with Edgar Percival in Mew Gull G-AFAA third.

The following month Lewin and his wife spent ten days in the Nile swamp after the Whitney Straight ran out of fuel during a flight home to Kenya before being rescued by a contingent of Sudanese troops.

At the annual general meeting of the Cardiff Aeroplane Club a healthy profit was reported and the decision made to increase the club's share capital to £5,000 by the issue of a further 3,000 £1 shares. At that time the club's flying rates were £2 0s 0d dual and £1 5s 0d solo on the Moths and £2 5s 0d dual and £1 15s 0d on the Hawk with reductions for guaranteed hours contracted in advance. Although reasonable by the standards of the day such prices would have been beyond the means of the average working man. That situation was soon to change, however.

In October 1937 Capt. C.D. Godfrey passed his test for his A licence at his first attempt and was able to join his sons Paul and Michael in flying his B.A. Swallow.

The year ended on a sad note with the untimely death, following an operation for appendicitis, of the club's chairman, Charles H. Keen, at the early age of thirty-six.

By 1938, the year of the Munich crisis, Britain's increasing military preparations were becoming ever more apparent no more so than at Pengam where the presence of No.614 (County of Glamorgan) Squadron Auxiliary Air Force had effectively turned the airport into a joint military/civil aerodrome.

From that year the annual air pageant, previously a largely civil affair, was superceded by Empire Air Day celebrations consisting of flying displays of a totally military nature and flypasts over South Wales of large formations of RAF aeroplanes, the sole civil participation being public joy riding. Those events will be covered under the appropriate heading.

It was a regular officer of 614 Squadron, Flt Lt H.T. Ferrand, who piloted Mr S.K. Davies' Gull in the 1938 Kings Cup Air Race, run as a closed circuit event at Hatfield. He was unplaced. In July the club fleet was augmented by the acquisition of Foster Wickner Wicko G.M.1 G-AEZZ, a two-seat high wing cabin monoplane powered by a 130hp Gipsy Major engine. A similar machine, G-AFKU, was purchased at the same time by local private owner Mr F.L. Dean. Both the Gull and the club Wicko piloted by Mr S.K. Davies and Capt. W.R. Bailey respectively, attended the Deauville Air Rally on 16 July, the third intended participant, the Miles Hawk, flown by an unnamed club member turned back due to adverse weather. In August Capt. Bailey qualified as a flying instructor and apparently taught with the club on a part-time basis.

The eighth and last London-Cardiff race of the inter-war years was run in ideal conditions on Saturday 10 September 1938 when six aeroplanes left Heston on an extended course which went beyond Pengam to turning points at Porthcawl and Jersey Marine before turning back to the finishing line at Pengam.

First away was R.L. Porteous, flying a diminutive Chilton D.W.1, G-AESZ, nearly forty-one minutes ahead of Geoffrey de Havilland junior in the T.K.2 G-ADNO. The handicapping was of the usual high standard, all of the competitors overflying Pengam in the order of departure, the Chilton being pursued by H.D. Rankin in Hawker Tomtit G-AFFL, L.I. Arnott in the Cardiff Aeroplane Club Wicko, H.J. Wilson in C.S. Napier's Gull Four G-ADOE, R.A. Winter's Gipsy engined Comper Swift and finally the T.K.2 whose over-rich engine emitted a spectacular trail of black smoke. The Chilton still led at Swansea but the Gull had moved up to second place ahead of the Wicko. The Swift was fourth, the T.K.2 fifth while the Tomtit brought up the rear. At the finish. the T.K.2 crossed the line twenty-seven seconds ahead of the Gull to score its third win in the event and de Havilland's second, R.A. Winter and L.I. Arnott in third and fourth places finished within two and a half minutes of the winner followed by the Chilton and the Tomtit in that order.

In 1938 the government, mindful of a possible requirement for a body of trained non-combatant pilots in the event of the outbreak of hostilities, founded the Civil Air Guard. The organisation, open to suitable men and women between the ages of eighteen and fifty, offered subsidised flying training at recognised flying clubs at rates between 2s 6d and 5s per hour on weekdays and between 5s and 10s per hour at weekends. Members were to be trained to A licence standard and allowed ten hours subsidised flying per annum thereafter. The plan was announced at the beginning of July and, needless to say, the response from the public was overwhelming, with over 35,000 applications being received nation-wide and 800 by the Cardiff Aeroplane Club alone.

Training commenced on 1 September 1938 for those in possession of A licences and on 1 October for *ab initio* students. Figures released in January 1939 revealed that 6,000 members had been enrolled nationally of whom 3,700, including 299 women, were under training at sixty clubs, and had already accomplished 20,000 hours of Civil Air Guard training. Cardiff Aeroplane Club already had forty-four Civil Air Guard pilots under training by December 1938, standardising training on the Pobjoy-engined B.A. Swallow, one of which, G-ADPS, joined the fleet in November 1938 to be joined by two more – G-AEIH and G-AFGD – in January 1939. However, owing to the waterlogged state of the aerodrome surface all three must have been inactive until March 1939.

Letters appearing in the aviation press at that time seemed to suggest that an uneasy relationship existed in some clubs between established club members and members of the Civil Air Guard but whether such a state of affairs appertained at Cardiff is impossible to tell. Hitherto, most flying clubs had been the exclusive preserve of members of the middle and upper classes at a time when the class structure still counted for a great deal. It would appear that many resented the intrusion into their world of the hoi polloi in their Civil Air Guard boilersuit-type uniforms just as much as members of the Civil Air Guard resented being patronised and sometimes segregated. Nevertheless the scheme was an outstanding success from the Government's point of view and also opened up the skies to many who could otherwise only have dreamed of flying.

The Cardiff Aeroplane Club continued to thrive throughout the summer of 1939. In June yet another Pobjoy-engined Swallow, G-AEAU, bought by Capt. C.D. Godfrey, appeared at Pengam as a replacement for G-AEOZ which had been disposed of. Finally, after a long wait the club was able to replace its aging D.H.60 Moths with brand new D.H.82 Tiger Moths after the De Havilland Co. had satisfied a large RAF order. Delivered in July 1939 they served for less than two months before they too were impressed into RAF service along with most other civil aeroplanes of the time.

15
The Flying Circuses, 1933–1936

As has been previously mentioned, the early part of the 1930s was the heyday of the flying circus, a concept pioneered in the United Kingdom by Capt. C.D. Barnard in 1931 and emulated by Sir Alan Cobham and M.A. Ap Rhys-Pryce the following year.

The circuses were in effect groups of barnstorming pilots, either companies or individuals, grouped around a central organising company. Besides joy riding, which remained the main source of income, the paying public was treated to a programme of events including aerobatics, gliding, wing-walking and parachuting along with various comedy and novelty items. Some of the stunts were quite breathtaking, Sir Alan Cobham's chief display pilots Geoffrey Tyson and Idwal Jones' displays of 'looping the hoop' – looping a Tiger Moth around a rope suspended between two poles, and picking a handkerchief off the ground with a hook attached to the Tiger Moth's wing tip being two worthy of mention.

The circuses toured the country between April and October staging two performances daily at up to 180 different venues, a major feat of logistics for the ground support teams who had to transport all ground equipment from site to site overnight.

Although performances were sometimes staged at aerodromes the majority took place in farmer's fields or other open spaces, many of which were small and often far from level.

Although both Barnard's Aerial Circus and Ap Rhys-Pryce's Crimson Fleet disbanded after only one year's operations, Sir Alan Cobham's National Aviation Day Display prospered and was joined from 1933 onwards by a rival organisation or perhaps one should say organisations established by two entrepreneurs by the names of Harry Barker and Jimmy McEwen King. The activities of Barker and McEwen King were somewhat convoluted as they involved a number of companies and the display's name was changed on an annual basis. Barker and McEwen King invariably remained in the background, their displays being fronted by famous fliers of the day.

For the 1933 season Sir Alan Cobham fielded a total of eighteen aircraft divided into two separate but virtually identical fleets the composition of which varied from time to time depending on serviceability and the nature of the landing grounds available.

Each fleet consisted of a Handley Page Airliner (either a H.P. W10 or H.P.33 Clive), an Airspeed Ferry, a D.H.82 Tiger Moth, a D.H.60 Moth, a Cierva C.19 Mk. IV Autogiro, a D.H.83 Fox Moth, a Blackburn Lincock Fighter, a Spartan Three Seater, and a number of Avro 504Ks supported by a fleet of Armstrong Siddeley motor vehicles and a fuel bowser.

The circus visited Glamorgan in May, performing at the Cross Hill field, Margam, on 24 May, Lock's Common, Porthcawl on 27 May, and Wenvoe Aerodrome on 28 May. The choice of the latter venue was dictated by the refusal of Cardiff City Council to permit the use of the municipal aerodrome for public entertainment on the Sabbath.

The following month the citizens of Swansea were treated to a similar display by the rival organisation trading that year as British Hospitals Air Pageants which visited Parc le Breos Farm near Penmaen, Gower, on Whit Monday and Tuesday, 5 and 6 June. They flew from a large field adjoining the A4118 road to the east of the farm access road.

The organisation was established with notable patrons too numerous to mention with the object of making money, a proportion of which was donated to local hospitals. The circus leader was Mr C.W.A. Scott AFC famous at the time as the holder of the England-Australia record and later to achieve even greater fame as the winner of the two great long distance air races: Mildenhall to Melbourne in 1934, and Portsmouth to Johannesburg in 1936. The fleet, which seemed to vary considerably from time to time, consisted of up to fifteen aircraft including examples of D.H.84 Dragon, Gipsy Moth, Fox Moth, Fairey Fox, Monospar, Desoutter, Miles Satyr, Bristol Trainers, Spartan Three Seaters, and of course, Avro 504s.

The pageant was declared open by the Mayor of Swansea (Cllr Daniel Evans JP) who, along with his wife, subsequently flew with Mr Scott. The pageant was an unqualified success, the only untoward event being when one of the participating aircraft shed its engine cowling into Caswell Bay from where it was subsequently recovered by a bathing attendant.

Times were obviously very good for the circus proprietors as figures released at the end of the season revealed. Of 800,000 who had paid admission to National Aviation Day Displays, 194,000 had flown. Of a similar number who had attended British Hospitals Air Pageants events, some 70,000 had flown, 6,000 in Pauline Gower's Spartan Three Seater and 8,000 in a similar aircraft of Capt. Percival Phillips DFC of the Cornwall Aviation Co. A total of £6,854 6s 10d was raised for hospitals.

In 1934 Barker and McEwen King formed a new company, Air Pageants Ltd, but operated under the banner of the Sky Devils Air Circus as before, undertaking to donate money (ten per cent of the gross take) to a selected hospital in each district. The magazine *Flight* gave the fleet as Armstrong Whitworth Argosy G-EBLF *City of Glasgow*, piloted by Capt. E.B. Fielden of Aviation Tours Ltd, converted to carry twenty-eight passengers, three Avro 504Ks and one each of Miles Hawk, Avro Tutor and a D.H.60 Moth (C.W.A. Scott's England to Australia record-breaking aeroplane). Cobham's fleet consisted of one Handley Page Clive, three Avro 640 Cadets with two-seat front cockpits, and one each of Airspeed Ferry, Cierva C.19 Mk. IV Autogiro, Blackburn Lincock, Tiger Moth, Avro 504K and Rhönbussard glider, the mount of Miss Joan Meakin, who had arrived in the country on 5 April after a 600 mile aero tow from Germany.

The Sky Devils made their first appearance in the county on 3 June at Wenvoe Aerodrome, presumably for the same reason that Sir Alan Cobham had used the site the previous year. The event was attended by good weather and a large crowd but did not meet with universal acclaim. The *Western Mail* of 14 July contained a lengthy letter of protest describing the display as, among other things '...a positive menace to the moral and spiritual life of the people'. It was signed by the Rt Revd T. Rees MA, Lord Bishop of Llandaff, along with eighty-six clergymen representing Anglican, Presbyterian, Congregational, Methodist and Baptist Churches, Capt. R.T. Evans MP, Mr O. Temple-Morris MP, Mr Patrick Munroe MP and sixty-two other signatories representing local political parties, the Cardiff and District Sunday School Union, the Federation of Sisterhoods, the Cardiff and District Federation of Brotherhoods, the Cardiff and District Temperance Union, the Salvation Army, the Barry Council of Evangelical Churches, the Sailors and Soldiers Rest, the British Women's Total Abstinence Union, the British and Foreign Bible Society and, of course, the Lord's Day Observance Society.

Aeroplanes of the Sky Devils Flying Circus in formation near Wenvoe on 3 June 1934. In the fore-ground is Avro 504N G-ACNV and behind is an Avro Tutor, probably G-ACOV. (Stan Reynolds)

Unabashed, the Sky Devils displayed with a fleet of only four aeroplanes at Cogan Hall Farm, Penarth, on 17 August, H.W. Ward's two parachute descents that evening being much appreciated.

What the Sky Devils could do, National Aviation Day could do better, or so it seemed. On 25 September, Ivor Price, the circus parachutist, using a series of Russell Lobe parachutes, made eight descents in fifteen minutes and fifty seconds from the Tiger Moth flown by Geoffrey Tyson during the circus' visit to Pengam Aerodrome.

The following day the circus performed for the only time in Barry from a field belonging to Walter's Farm adjacent to Port Road. The field, later known as The Gunsite, is now a part-ly developed area immediately to the south of the present Tesco supermarket. The display was severely hampered by high winds and heavy showers and several events had to be abandoned. The circus moved on to Cross Hill field, Margam, on 27 September.

As the year 1935 was the Silver Jubilee of King George V and Queen Mary, Air Pageants Ltd adopted the title of Jubilee Air Displays for that season. The circus that year being front-ed by Owen Cathcart-Jones and Capt. Tommy Campbell-Black.

Both men had achieved fame in October 1934 as competitors in the Mac Robertson Mildenhall to Melbourne air race. Campbell-Black had partnered C.W.A. Scott in the win-ning D.H.88 Comet in the then astonishing time of seventy hours fifty-four minutes, while Cathcart-Jones and his partner Ken Waller, having flown another Comet into fourth place, immediately set out on the return journey and established an out and return record of thir-teen and a half days.

The Jubilee Air Display performed at the Vennaway Lane field at Parkmill, Gower, on 8 June, Lock's Common, Porthcawl, on 9 June, and spent Whit Monday and Tuesday, 10 and

11 June, at Wenvoe Aerodrome. All the displays, it appears, were severely affected by adverse weather.

By contrast the display by National Aviation Day at Pengam on 25 September was blessed by perfect conditions and drew a record crowd but, as with the Jubilee Air Display, the performance at Vennaway Lane on the 26 September was marred by low cloud and drizzle.

By the end of 1935, the end was in sight for the flying circuses. Sir Alan Cobham, shrewd as ever, sold National Aviation Day Display, with the exception of the name, to C.W.A. Scott who traded as C.W.A. Scott's Flying For All Display. The display did not visit the district during the 1936 season at the end of which the company went into receivership and was eventually wound up.

Barker and McEwen King continued to operate during the 1936 season under the title Campbell-Black's British Empire Air Display, which was somewhat of a misnomer as Campbell-Black only joined the tour at weekends flying his black and silver Puss Moth. Other aircraft included Spartan Three Seater, Avro 504N, Hawker Tomtit, Flying Flea and Short Scion. The fleet performed at Pengam on Saturday 25 July where in perfect weather conditions the show went off without a hitch.

That was more than could be said of the following day's performance at Lock's Common, Porthcawl, when the Short Scion G-ADDT, which was returning from a joy ride with five passengers aboard, struck telephone wires and crashed into a field behind houses in Windsor Road.

The pilot R.F. Robinson was thrown through the cockpit roof by the force of the impact and was subsequently conveyed to Bridgend District Hospital. Finding the cabin door jammed, the passengers, who suffered only minor injuries, made good their escape through the hole in the roof so conveniently made by their unfortunate pilot.

Sadly Campbell-Black was killed in a bizarre taxiing accident at Speke Airport, Liverpool, on 19 September 1936 whilst on business unconnected with the circus. The company ceased trading at the end of the year and, although its proprietors set up yet another company in 1937, its activities were confined in the main to Ireland before it too went into liquidation at the end of the year. The era of the flying circus had come to an end.

The reasons for their demise can only be guessed at. Maybe the public demand had been satiated. Maybe aviation had become too commonplace or maybe with an ever-increasing number of new aerodromes putting on their own air pageants, the circuses no longer filled a need.

Whatever the reasons, a phenomenon that thrilled millions throughout the land and provided memories that endured for decades ended forever.

16
The Giant Airships

Many older people are likely to recall the occasion when the giant airship flew over South Wales, many insisting it to have been the ill-fated R.101 wrecked with great loss of life in October 1930. However, after extensive research I can state with some confidence that that particular airship was never seen over Glamorgan although a number of others were.

Known as rigid airships due to their mode of construction, they owed their origin to the work of a retired German army officer by the name of Count Ferdinand von Zeppelin whose name, like that of W.H. Hoover, tended to become synonymous with all similar products regardless of manufacturer. Unlike the smaller non-rigid airships, whose envelopes relied on gas pressure to maintain their shape, the rigid craft's massive hulls consisted of a fabric-covered framework of immense complexity containing numerous separate gas cells to which the forward control cabin and a number of engine cars accommodating both engines and engineers were attached. Accommodation for passengers in early examples was a railway coach-like structure below the hull, but later commercial ships boasted spacious cabins and state rooms incorporated into the lower part of the hull itself.

Von Zeppelin's original design, the 420ft long LZ.1 completed in 1900, was the largest aircraft of its day and for the next four decades the Zeppelin Co. and others constructed airships of ever greater size culminating in craft whose awesome proportions almost defy the imagination of people, the author included, too young to have seen one. *

Early progress was such that by 1909 Zeppelin airships had entered commercial service. Between then and the outbreak of hostilities a fleet that ultimately numbered six ships made some 1,600 flights and transported over 35,000 passengers on German internal air services.

During the First World War about 100 airships of both Zeppelin and Schütte-Lanz design were produced for the German naval and military air services for use in reconnaissance and bombing roles. Raids were mounted against targets on the East Coast and in the English Midlands but due to increasingly sophisticated defence tactics and the aid of the British weather, little damage of significance to the war effort was done although about 500 people, mainly civilians, perished as a result of the campaign.

British rigid airship development lagged far behind that of Germany, the only pre-war example, the 512ft long *Mayfly*, being wrecked at Barrow-in-Furness in September 1911 having never flown. Further examples were produced in the latter half of the war but none played a significant part in hostilities.

It was one such ship, HM Airship R.36, that was almost certainly the first rigid airship to be seen from Glamorgan when she cruised up the Bristol Channel in the evening of 11 June 1921.

---

* For those who, like the author, find the dimensions of those aerial leviathans difficult to comprehend, a few comparisons may be of assistance. A Boeing 747 'Jumbo Jet' is 231ft long, that familiar summer sight in the Bristol Channel, the PS *Waverley* is 240ft, Penarth Pier 658ft, while the height of the St Hilary television mast is 745ft.

HM Airship R.36.
(The Airship
Heritage Trust)

In terms of sheer volume, the R.36 must rank as one of the biggest white elephants ever produced in the history of the British aerospace industry. Built by Beardmores of Inchinnan, she was still under construction when the armistice was signed. Declared surplus to military requirements she was ordered to be completed as a commercial airship by somebody in authority whose grasp of mathematics must have been, to say the least, minimal. Although quite a large airship: she was 675ft long, 78ft maximum diameter with a gas capacity of 2,101,000cu.ft – a few simple calculations should have revealed the utter impracticality of the idea.

After the fitting of a coach-like fifty-seat passenger compartment complete with cabins and all domestic necessities, her lifting capacity was effectively halved. The Air Ministry's boast that she could lift a payload of thirty passengers plus a ton of cargo *and* sufficient fuel to fly non-stop to Egypt was correct as far as it went. The problem was she couldn't do both at the same time! Allotted the civil registration G-FAAF she made her first flight, appropriately enough on 1 April 1921, and was positioned to Pulham, Norfolk, the following day from where she made, as far as can be ascertained, only about half a dozen flights.

On the one in question she slipped her moorings at 10.07 a.m. on 10 June and cruised as far as Land's End conducting radio navigation trials. She was seen by thousands of South Walians as she cruised up the Bristol Channel between 8.15 p.m. and 9.00 p.m. on 11 June heading back to Pulham where she moored early the following morning. Only ten days later she was damaged in a mooring accident and after about five years in storage, scrapped.

The R.36 fiasco, if it did nothing else, served to demonstrate a fundamental fact. An airship capable of transporting a large number of passengers and freight over a long distance must have a substantial margin between the available lift, governed by the amount of gas contained, and the basic weight of its structure. The margin represents the lift available for passengers, cargo and of course fuel which governs the airship's range. In other words, a long-range airship has to be very big.

Between the wars a number of such ships were constructed, mainly in Germany and the United Kingdom and South Walians saw several of them.

The first truly successful example was the German LZ.127 the 'Graf Zeppelin', completed in 1928. With a length of 775ft, a diameter of 100ft and containing 4,000,000cu.ft of hydrogen, nearly double that of the R.36, she was capable of carrying a crew of thirty-seven and

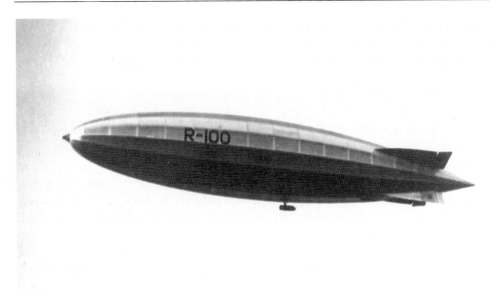

HM Airship R.100. (The Airship Heritage Trust)

twenty passengers on transatlantic journeys with ease and was used successfully on a non-stop service between Germany and Rio de Janeiro for many years, something that nobody at that time could envisage an aeroplane ever being able to accomplish. During her twelve-year life she circled the globe, made 144 Atlantic crossings, flew over a million miles and carried 18,000 passengers. She was, without doubt, the most successful long-range airship ever built.

In the United Kingdom too, thoughts turned to an airship service reaching out to the furthest parts of the Empire, resulting in orders being placed for two giant airships, the R.100, constructed by the Airship Guarantee Co., a Vickers subsidiary at Howden, Yorkshire, and the R.101 built by the Royal Airship Works, Cardington, Bedfordshire. Sadly, the project developed serious political overtones beyond the scope of this work, but suffice it to say the government-built R.101 made her first flight from Cardington on 14 October 1929, followed by the privately built R.100 from Howden on 16 December of the same year.

Both ships underwent flight trials from Cardington; the ill-designed and ill-starred R.101 made a total of eleven such flights during 1929 and 1930, none of which brought her near South Wales. The R.100, however, was in the area during her trials but whether she was visible from the ground due to prevailing cloud conditions is difficult to determine.

She was a large ship, shorter than the *Graf Zeppelin* at 709ft, but her diameter of 133ft allowed a greater gas capacity of 5,156,000cu.ft. A further concession to her disposable load was the choice of power plant, six 660hp Rolls-Royce Condor aeroplane engines which, running on petrol instead of the heavier diesel fuel, favoured by most large airship designers, allowed a saving in fuel weight of close on five tons.

She may well have been visible from South Wales during her fifth flight, an endurance trial that lasted for two days, six hours and fifty-two minutes between 27 and 29 January 1930. Although much of the trial, which took in a large part of the country, was conducted in cloud, she did route down the Bristol Channel in clear air from Bristol to Lundy between

12.20 p.m. and 1.50 p.m. on 27 January and carried out turning trials, also in clear air, north of Minehead on 29 January. She also passed down the Bristol Channel on her seventh trial on the night of 25/26 July 1930 but as it was dark and most of the flight was conducted in cloud she probably passed unnoticed.

The flight of the R.100 that most people remember was her triumphant return from Canada following her successful crossing from Cardington to Dorval, Montreal, between 29 July and 1 August 1930. After a sojourn in Canada, during which she flew about twenty-five hours, the return journey commenced at 1.30 a.m. GMT on 14 August.

Commanded by Sqn Ldr R.S. Booth with Capt. George Meager, the former captain of SR.1, as second in command, her compliment of fifty-six passengers and crew included her designer, Dr Barnes Wallis, more well remembered today for his work on the dam busting bouncing bomb, and her assistant designer Mr N.S. Norway, better known by his *nom de plume* Nevil Shute, the bestselling novelist.

She made her landfall at Fastnet in the early hours of 16 August, was overhead Lundy at 6.45 a.m. GMT, south of Mumbles at 7.00 a.m., and south of Barry and Cardiff at 7.45 a.m. To quote the *South Wales Echo*: 'The spectacle caused great excitement and interrupted many shaves and breakfasts.' She subsequently overflew Avonmouth and moored at Cardington at 10.35 a.m. after a flight of fifty-seven hours and five minutes.

To all concerned it must have seemed to be the dawning of a new age in British commercial air travel, but it was not to be. The thousands who watched the R.100's majestic progress up-channel that morning could not have known that they were witnessing not a great beginning but the end of a chapter. It was in fact the last successful flight by a British rigid airship.

On 4 October 1930 her rival, for that is what she had become, the R.101 as the result of the triumph of political dogma over common sense left Cardington for India on a journey that with both foresight and hindsight was doomed from the start. In the early hours of 5 October she met a fiery end on a hillside near Beauvais, with the loss of forty-eight lives including Lord Thomson, the Air Minister, at whose feet most of the true blame lay, and the majority of the protagonists of the British airship programme.

The ensuing public horror, coupled with the loss of so many of the prime movers, led to the abandonment of the entire scheme. The R.100 never flew again and was broken up.

The R.100 was not, however, the last rigid airship to be seen over Glamorgan, for Germany kept faith with the concept for many more years. The *Graf Zeppelin* paid several visits to Britain in the 1930s and on one such occasion, 2 July 1932 arrived at Hanworth Air Park, London, from her base at Friedrichshafen, disembarked thirty-five German passengers, embarked about twenty British ones and set off on a twenty-four-hour cruise around Britain. The cruise, variously described as a wonderful experience and a trial for smokers, encompassed the Isle of Wight, the west of Scotland, the Isle of Man and a routing via Liverpool and the Welsh Marches to Newport and Cardiff where the *Graf Zeppelin* appeared unexpectedly flying at about 1,500ft just below the cloudbase at 3.30 p.m. on the afternoon of 3 July. She passed directly over Lower Penarth, Cadoxton and the centre of Barry before turning south and disappearing from view into the cloudy sky over the Bristol Channel. Flg-Off. Bunning and George Watkiss of the Cardiff Aeroplane Club on seeing the airship, took off in the club's Gipsy Moth and gave chase.

This photograph taken by Mr J.W. Frampton shows the Graf Zeppelin over Barry Docks on 3 July 1932. (Mr H.K. Frampton)

They were able to get close enough to make out the captain, Dr Hugo Eckener, probably the greatest rigid commander of all time, seated in the control cabin reading a newspaper – plus ça change!

The last, and largest, rigid to enter commercial service was the LZ.129, the *Hindenburg*. First flown in 1936 she was 809ft long, 135ft diameter and of 7,000,000cu.ft capacity. She entered service between Frankfurt and New York overflying the UK regularly until the British Government correctly suspecting the motives for such overflights, prohibited all German airships from UK airspace except when severe weather conditions dictated otherwise.

She was probably visible on two occasions from Glamorgan – once in the late evening of 13 May 1936 when she passed just to the north of the county boundary on a track that took her near Carmarthen and Brecon as she routed inbound from the United States and again in the early evening of 5 July when she passed up the Bristol Channel. Her destruction by fire while mooring at Lakehurst, New Jersey, so dramatically captured on film, on 6 May 1937 was to most people's minds one airship accident too many and effectively put an end to further development.

In any case the big rigids, like the dinosaurs, had had their day as the tremendous strides made in the development of long range aeroplanes in the latter years of the decade were beginning to bear fruit. However, it seems that nobody who worked with them or saw one will ever forget them.

17
Air Transport

In 1933 the directors of the GWR decided that the time was ripe to exercise powers granted to all four railway companies in 1929 and commence scheduled air services. The powers had been sought and granted to exclude the possibility, envisaged with extraordinary foresight, that at some future date internal air transport operators, of whom there were none at that time, might pose the same sort of competitive threat to mainline railway services as the expanding motor omnibus companies were already posing to branch line services.

For their first tentative foray into air transport the GWR decided on a route from Cardiff via Haldon (with road connections to Torquay, Newton Abbot and Teignmouth) to Plymouth (Roborough) Aerodrome. They chose the route, as Norman Edgar did, reasoning that, although contemporary transport aeroplanes were not significantly faster than express trains, they did possess a significant advantage in terms of journey times where crossing bodies of water, such as the Bristol Channel, were concerned.

To facilitate the operation the company entered into agreement with Imperial Airways Ltd who undertook to provide an aeroplane, pilots and engineering support while the GWR maintained responsibility for bookings, surface transport and the provision of traffic staff. The aeroplane assigned to the service was a Westland Wessex, powered by three Armstrong Siddeley Genet Major engines, bearing, by complete coincidence, the very appropriate registration letters G-AAGW. For the duration of the six month lease it was finished in the GWR's familiar chocolate and cream colour scheme, its six-seat cabin being appointed in the style of a first class railway compartment. The two pilots assigned to the service were the veteran Capts G.P. Olley and F. 'Dizzy' Dismore.

Two daily return services were scheduled; the timetables, like all pre-war railway air service timetables, displayed a distinctly railway-orientated approach with very short turn-around times – times that, for all manner of reasons, no present day airline operator could hope to equal.

The morning service departed Cardiff at 9.15 a.m., arrived at Haldon at 10.05 a.m. and, after a five minute turnaround, continued to Plymouth where it arrived at 10.35 a.m. The return service left Plymouth at 11.25 a.m. and arrived back at Cardiff at 12.50 p.m. The afternoon service followed the same pattern leaving Cardiff at 1.35 p.m. and arriving back at 5.20 p.m. Passengers were checked in and subsequently deposited at the appropriate railway stations which, due to the close proximity of the aerodromes to the urban areas, meant only short journeys by surface transport. The savings in time were considerable, about three hours being cut from the Cardiff-Plymouth rail journey, but the fares were high. Cardiff to Teignmouth cost £3 single and £5 return, as compared with £1 8s 6d single and £2 17s return first class rail. The fares to Plymouth were £3 10s single and £6 return, compared with £1 16s 5d and £3 12s 10d. Although children under three travelled free, the children's half price fare only applied to those between the ages of three and seven. The free baggage allowance was 35lb. with a surcharge of 6d per lb thereafter, although heavy luggage could be conveyed by rail free of charge.

Following the inaugural flight on 11 April, when the Wessex piloted by Capt Olley and escorted, it seems, by several other aeroplanes, flew the route carrying senior railway officials and a *Western Mail* reporter, the service opened to the public the following day. Demand proved to be far from high, however, and from 15 May the fares were reduced to £2 single and £3 12s return to Teignmouth and £2 5s and £4 single and return respectively to Plymouth. From that day also mail was carried, to be posted on arrival with a 3d surcharge.

Quite suddenly the company changed its tactics and from 22 May moved its terminus to Birmingham (Castle Bromwich) Aerodrome from where it mounted a daily return service via Cardiff and Haldon to Plymouth. The aeroplane departed Birmingham at 9.30 a.m., arrived at Cardiff at 10.40 a.m., departing at 11.00 a.m. to arrive at Haldon at 11.50 a.m. and Plymouth at 12.20 p.m. The return service was timed to leave Plymouth at 4.00 p.m. arriving at Cardiff at 5.20 p.m. and Birmingham at 6.50 p.m. The Cardiff-Birmingham fare was set at £2 single and £3 15s return, nearly double the first class rail fare. The timings seemed to be designed to appeal more to Birmingham passengers wishing to visit Wales and the West Country rather than vice versa.

The service terminated for the season on 30 September having incurred a heavy financial loss but having also demonstrated the feasibility of internal airline services from the operational aspect. During the six-month period, despite a complete lack of en route or terminal navigation aids, only four services were cancelled, two due to adverse weather and two due to technical defects – a remarkable achievement.

Norman Edgar too could look back on a year of continued success with his Bristol-Cardiff ferry service due, no doubt, in part to the decision taken in June to reduce fares to 9s single and 18s return, less than the first class rail fare. Demand had frequently been such that the Fox Moth sometimes had to be backed up by a second aeroplane, presumably a company Puss Moth. In September a new company Norman Edgar (Western Airways) had been formed by

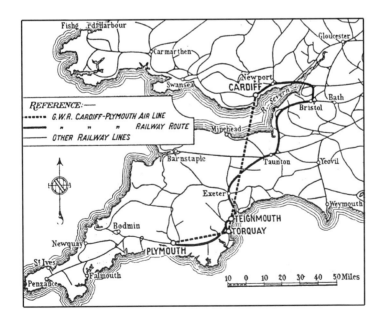

Route map of Great Western Railway, Cardiff-Plymouth service, summer 1933.

		First Service.		Second Service.	
		a.m.		p.m.	
Cardiff General Station	*dep. by* 'Bus	9.0	—	1.30	—
Cardiff Air Port	*arr.* ,, ,,	9.10	—	1.40	—
		a.m.		p.m.	
Cardiff Air Port	*dep.* ,, 'Plane	—	9.15	—	1.45
Haldon Aerodrome	*arr.* ,, ,,	—	10.5	—	2.35
Haldon Aerodrome	*dep.* ,, ,,	—	10.10	—	2.40
Roborough Aerodrome	*arr.* ,, ,,	—	10.35	—	3.5
Plymouth North Road Station	*arr.* ,, 'Bus	10.55	—	3.25	—
Plymouth North		a.m.		p.m.	
Road Station	*dep. by* 'Bus	11.0	—	3.30	—
Roborough Aerodrome	*arr.* ,, ,,	11.20	—	3.50	—
Roborough			a.m.		p.m.
Aerodrome	*dep.* ,, 'Plane	—	11.25	—	3.55
Haldon Aerodrome	*arr.* ,, ,,	—	11.50	—	4.20
Haldon Aerodrome	*dep.* ,, ,,	—	noon 12.0	—	4.30
Cardiff Air Port	*arr.* ,, ,,	—	p.m. 12.50	—	5.20
Cardiff General Station	*arr.* ,, 'Bus	p.m. 1.0	—	5.30	—

The motor 'bus service between Haldon Aerodrome, Teignmouth and Torquay, is as follows :—

		a.m.	a.m.	p.m.	p.m.
Torquay Station	.. *dep.*	9.0	10.50	1.35	3.20
Torquay Vaughan Parade	*dep.*	9.5	10.55	1.40	3.25
Teignmouth Enquiry Bureau	*dep.*	9.35	11.25	2.10	3.55
Haldon Aerodrome	.. *arr.*	9.55	11.45	2.25	4.10
Haldon Aerodrome	.. *dep.*	10.10	noon 12.0	2.40	4.30
Teignmouth Enquiry Bureau	*arr.*	10.20	p.m. 12.10	2.50	4.40
Torquay Vaughan Parade	*arr.*	10.50	12.40	3.20	5.10

Timetable for Great Western Railway, Cardiff-Plymouth service, summer 1933.

Advertisement for Norman Edgar (Western Airways) Cardiff-Bristol ferry, June 1933. (Author's collection)

D.H. Dragon City of Cardiff *of Railway Air Services.* (Kenneth G. Wakefield)

Edgar and two other directors and had taken delivery of an eight-passenger D.H.84 Dragon I G-ACJT. Two new pilots, Capts C.R. Cubitt and G.W. Monk, had been employed and over a thousand passengers had used the service in the twelve months to 31 December. As was the case previously, the ferry continued to operate throughout the winter months.

By the end of the year the licensed area of Pengam had increased to fifty-three acres and further work was in hand to increase it to eighty acres. The aerodrome boasted four grass runways of 600 yards north-south, 450 yards northeast-southwest, 630 yards east-west and 600 yards southeast-northwest. A new approach road had been built from Whitaker Road to the hangar together with a car park for 200 cars. The addition of a custom house led to the council deciding in May 1934 to refer to the aerodrome as Cardiff Airport.

The acquisition of the Dragon greatly increased Western Airways' potential, allowing the carriage of more passengers at a lower cost-per-seat mile than hitherto. It also allowed the company to pioneer what has become so much a part of modern day Welsh life – the rugby airlift. On 20 January the Bristol-Cardiff ferry ran an hourly service carrying English supporters to Cardiff for the Wales *v.* England rugby international. On 3 February a less successful attempt at Wales' first rugby charter was mounted when Capt. Cubitt left Cardiff for Edinburgh carrying eight miners from Tylerstown, who came to be known as 'The Tylerstown Eight' to watch the Wales *v.* Scotland match.

Unfortunately, weather conditions over the Midlands were such that Cubitt was forced to turn back, but The Eight, determined to enjoy the weekend for which they had undoubtedly saved, persuaded him to overfly Cardiff and continue to Portsmouth where they watched a match, played with the other shaped ball, between Portsmouth and Sheffield United. After a night out in Portsmouth they landed back in Cardiff on Sunday having first overflown Tylerstown, no doubt greatly cheered by their country's crushing defeat of the Scots, and vowed to try again the following year.

Finally on 24 February the Dragon ferried forty officials and supporters of Bristol Rovers Football Club to Cardiff for a match against Cardiff City.

Meanwhile throughout the winter all four railway companies together with Imperial Airways and others entered into complex negotiations with the objective of establishing an airline to operate an extensive internal route network. The outcome was Railway Air Services, RAS for short, registered on 21 March 1934 owned jointly by the four companies and Imperial Airways. The internal financial and operational arrangements were complex due largely to a curious anomaly brought about by a restriction in the 1929 act confining individual company flying operations to the areas covered by their rail network. That led to the company being split into several divisions. For the first time the company owned its own aeroplanes although the pilots were still seconded from Imperial Airways.

Among the first operations by RAS was the GWR division's daily return services from Plymouth via Haldon, Cardiff, Birmingham (Castle Bromwich) to Liverpool (Speke) using D.H.84 Dragon 2 G-ACPX. Following a proving flight on 4 May 1934 the service was opened to the public on 7 May. The aeroplane left Plymouth at 8.25 a.m. and arrived at Cardiff at 9.55 a.m. departing at 10.00 a.m. The returning flight arrived and departed Cardiff at 5.00 p.m. and 5.25 p.m. respectively. The service proved to be particularly useful to the producers of Devonshire cream which could be distributed to all stations en route within hours of manufacture.

D.H.84 Dragon 1 G-ACJT which went into service with the newly formed Norman Edgar (Western Airways) in September 1933. (Kenneth G. Wakefield)

From 30 July the direction of travel was reversed, the aeroplane leaving Liverpool at 8.45 a.m., arriving and departing Cardiff at 10.45 a.m. and 10.50 a.m. respectively, until the service terminated for the winter on 30 September. The more economical Dragon allowed a substantial reduction in fares, Cardiff-Plymouth, for example, being £2 2s single and £3 5s return.

Western Airways began to expand their sphere of operations by introducing a twice-daily Cardiff-Bristol-Bournemouth service which connected at Bournemouth with services operated by Portsmouth Southsea and Isle of Wight Aviation to Portsmouth the Isle of Wight and Brighton (Shoreham) and Jersey Airways services to Jersey. After a proving flight on 13 May, fare-paying passengers were carried from 17 May until that service closed for the winter on 30 September.

The service completed a link in a network of connecting air services branching from the main trunk of the RAS Plymouth-Liverpool route allowing passengers to travel almost the length and breadth of the UK. Besides the connections already mentioned, it was possible to change at Birmingham for Bristol and the Isle of Wight on a second RAS route or at Liverpool onto services of Midland and Scottish Air Ferries Ltd to the Isle of Man, Belfast and Glasgow.

Directors and pilots of Norman Edgar (Western Airways) in front of a D.H.84 Dragon I. Left to right: Norman Edgar, Capt. C.R. Cubitt, Capt G.W Monk and Lt Col. D.B. Gray OBE, MC. (Kenneth G. Wakefield)

Opposite: *Poster advertising Railway Air Services – Plymouth-Liverpool, Isle of Wight-Birmingham and London-Isle of Wight services of 1934.* (Welsh Industrial & Maritime Museum/Kenneth G. Wakefield)

RAILWAY AIR SERVICES

De Havilland Dragon 8-Seater Twin-Engined Aeroplane as operating on
the Plymouth—Liverpool and Cowes—Birmingham Services

PLYMOUTH, TEIGNMOUTH, CARDIFF BIRMINGHAM and LIVERPOOL.

COWES (I. of W.), SOUTHAMPTON BRISTOL, BIRMINGHAM.

LONDON (Croydon) and ISLE of WIGHT

Full information from any G.W.R. or S.R. Station
or Office, Principal L M S Stations
and Travel Agents.

D.H.89 Dragon Rapide G-ADDD of Western Airways, formerly the property of HRH The Prince of Wales, which the company acquired in May 1937. (Kenneth G. Wakefield)

On 20 August the Inland Air Mail Service was inaugurated and although appalling weather conditions hampered operations in many parts of the country more than 2,000 letters were conveyed from Cardiff to Bristol, Southampton and the Isle of Wight.

So reliable had Western Airways' Bristol-Cardiff ferry service became that it acquired its first season ticket holder Mr Llewellyn C. Wood, who commuted daily to work across the Bristol Channel.

In July Charles Keen, Capt. W.R. Bailey and others formed Bristol Channel Airways, a charter company equipped with a single, three-seat D.H.85 Leopard Moth which reportedly did good business until the aeroplane was sold at the end of the year to make way, so it was said, for a larger aeroplane.

The Tylerstown Eight mounted a second expedition on 9 March 1935 when they flew from Pengam to Belfast (Aldergrove) in a Western Airways Dragon piloted by Capt. Cubitt, to watch the Wales *v.* Ireland rugby international. The outbound trip on that occasion was without incident and having watched Wales lose by 9 points to 3 and spent the night in Belfast, they arrived at Aldergrove on Sunday morning to discover that Cubitt was loath to leave due to forecast gale force winds and snow showers.

At about 2.30 p.m., however, Cubitt deemed conditions suitable to make an attempt and set off for Cardiff routing overhead the Isle of Man. Once en route, however, the Dragon, whose cruising speed was only 95 knots encountered a headwind of over 60 knots and extensive snowstorms blocked the proposed route. After an unsuccessful attempt to circumnavigate the storms by routing towards southern Scotland only to encounter severe turbulence and icing, Cubitt as all good aviators must, realised that he was beaten and returned to Aldergrove where he landed after a flight of nearly two hours. The disembarking party presented such a pitiful spectacle to some passing RAF officers that a billet block was put at their disposal to rest and recuperate before returning to their Belfast Hotel.

The return journey was eventually accomplished via Liverpool on the Monday when such was the headwind that the flying time was nearly six hours. The Eight were at least able to take comfort in the fact that their ordeal was considerably less than that of their less adventurous countrymen whose Irish Sea ferries encountered gale force winds, snow and seas so mountainous that all passengers were ordered below decks and some captains ordered the issue of lifebelts.

Two significant events in the early part of the year were the installation at Pengam of a G.E.C. 9kw landing floodlight which opened the airport to night operations and the first moves towards establishing an aerodrome at Swansea. Swansea Corporation, like their counterparts in Cardiff, had heeded Sir Alan Cobham's advocacy of municipal aerodromes and the subject had first been raised in 1929, the preferred site being Fairwood Common. However the story in Swansea was one of procrastination that continued until the contingency of war finally rendered Fairwood Common Aerodrome a *fait accompli*. It therefore fell to private enterprise to make the necessary moves.

For some time an open grass area on Jersey Marine, adjacent to Swansea Bay Golf Club, had been in occasional use as a landing ground for light aeroplanes, flown in the main by members of the Cardiff Aeroplane Club. The idea of extending and levelling the area would appear to have been largely the idea of Capt. C.D. 'Skipper' Godfrey, a former master mariner and managing director of the Briton Ferry Tin Plate Co., who was an active member of both clubs.

Work appears to have commenced on the project in March 1935 and an air service linking Swansea to London's Heston Aerodrome by Bristol Channel Airways Ltd was proposed. To that end, the company evaluated a number of aeroplanes, a Short S.16 Scion, which may have visited Swansea, a D.H.84 Dragon which landed on the site on 30 March and a General

D.H.89 Dragon Rapide G-ADDD repainted in the colours of the Straight Corporation after its take-over of Western Airways in 1938. (Kenneth G. Wakefield)

D.H.89 of Railway Air Services. (Kenneth G. Wakefield)

Aircraft Monospar which flew in on 3 April. In the event the site did not receive Air Ministry approval until the following year by which time Bristol Channel Airways had faded into oblivion.

Another company formed at that time was Cambrian Air Services Ltd, registered on 25 April with directors: Col. R.G. Llewellyn, OBE, MC, JP of Neath; Mr S.K. Davies of Cardiff; and Mr G.H. Wilson-Fox. The objective of the company was to acquire a share-holding and ultimately some sort of control over the operation of Norman Edgar (Western Airways) Ltd.

Although successful in the first objective, some 700 Western Airways shares being acquired by the company and its directors, Cambrian Air Services Ltd made no significant contribution to Western Airways policy and, except for a few small commissions, presumably using the private aeroplanes of Mr S.K. Davies, played no significant part in pre-war Welsh aviation.

By the time RAS implemented their 1935 summer timetable their route structure had become more complex. The Plymouth service routed via the newly opened Denbury Aerodrome (a request stop for Torquay, Newton Abbot and Teignmouth), Cardiff, Birmingham (Castle Bromwich) to a new terminus at Nottingham (Tollerton). It was operated simultaneously in opposite directions by two D.H.84 Dragon 2s G-ADDI and G-ADDJ and ran from 27 May to 14 September. Another service, from Liverpool to Brighton (Shoreham) via Birmingham, Bristol, Southampton and Portsmouth, was served by a connecting service between Cardiff and Bristol by Western Airways who from May increased the frequency of the ferry from three to four services daily.

Western Airways also advertised a weekend service from Cardiff via Bristol and Bournemouth to Le Touquet and Paris (Le Bourget) between, as far as can be ascertained,

D.H.86B operated by Western Airways from April 1939 to the outbreak of war. (Kenneth G. Wakefield)

24 May and 30 September. The flight was timed to depart Cardiff at 4.00 p.m. on Friday and Paris at 4.00 p.m. on Sunday. Fares were £6 15s to Le Touquet and £7 5s to Paris. It is unclear whether the Western Airways aeroplane flew all the way or whether passengers were transferred to the service of another operator. In order to facilitate the expected increase in summer activity another aeroplane, D.H.84 Dragon 2 G-ACMP was leased from Jersey Airways and extra pilots employed.

Another aeroplane that became a familiar sight at Pengam from April 1935 onwards was the Short S.16 Scion I G-ACUW of Atlantic Coast Air Services, later renamed Lundy, and of Atlantic Coast Airlines, a Barnstaple-based carrier principally engaged in operating a ferry service to Lundy Island but who also undertook an on demand service to Cardiff.

After nearly three years of incident-free airline operations into and out of Pengam, disaster struck on 22 July 1935 when Western Airways-operated Dragon G-ACMP crashed while approaching the airport killing all three occupants. The aeroplane had left Bristol at 7.50 p.m. on the evening ferry flight under the command of Capt. J.G. Mansfield and was seen by Flg-Off. Cope and other members of the Cardiff Aeroplane Club approaching the airport on schedule flying at an estimated height of about 700ft. 'No passengers tonight,' remarked Cope, as the group watched the Dragon pull up into a climb of approximately 40 degrees consistent with an entry to a stall turn or wingover, a manoeuvre that no airline pilot, even in those days, would normally have attempted with passengers aboard. The group watched in fascinated horror as the aeroplane stalled, executed two turns of a spin to the right and plunged into about 2ft of water on the mudflats about a mile and a half from the airport 'with a mighty splash'.

Haymakers from Mardy Farm rushed to the scene and, working up to their armpits in mud and water, ripped the side out of the aeroplane and extricated the body of a man which was transferred to a motor boat that had arrived at the scene. Capt. W.R. Bailey who had by that time arrived overhead in his Moth indicated that there were more occupants and after further efforts a second body was recovered. Both men were taken to Cardiff Pier Head where they were pronounced dead. The rising tide then rendered all further rescue efforts impossible and in fact one would-be rescuer, a boy, became stuck in the mud and was only freed in the nick of time. Capt. Mansfield's body was recovered the following morning.

At the subsequent inquest evidence was given that the Dragon was in sound mechanical order up to the time of impact and that post mortem investigation had revealed no evidence of pilot incapacitation. Evidence from a member of Western Airways' Bristol ground staff, however, suggested that one of the passengers had been overheard enquiring if the pilot could perform aerobatic manoeuvres during the flight. Although conclusive evidence was obviously lacking it was the opinion of the Air Ministry Inspector of Accidents that 'the pilot executed a manoeuvre which caused the aircraft to stall and spin at a height insufficient to enable him to effect a complete recovery from the ensuing dive.' The jury returned an open verdict.

From 5 August Western Airways advertised a daily Cardiff-Paris service leaving Cardiff at 10.15 a.m. every morning, but this was almost certainly run in conjunction with another operator via Bournemouth. By August the company was operating three Dragons and at least two Puss Moths and at the end of a successful year undertook a major re-organisation of its structure.

On 12 December 1935 Norman Edgar and others formed Western Air Transport Ltd, the stated objects being to 'purchase such of the present and future debts due or owing or to become due and owing by Norman Edgar (Western Airways) Ltd of 40 Broad St, Bristol, as the company shall deem fit, to operate airlines.' It seems to have been a manoeuvre to avoid the unwanted influence on the company by the directors of Cambrian Air Services. The lease of the hangar at Pengam was transferred to the new company but the operation continued under the Western Airways name.

For a time it seemed that Cardiff Corporation's decision to site the aerodrome on the foreshore to cater for marine aircraft had been a wise one when talks were held with a view to Cardiff becoming a European terminal for the Pan American Airways pioneering trans-Atlantic flying boat service, but in the event they came to nothing.

The opening of Weston-super-Mare municipal aerodrome in 1936 had an effect on air transport in South Wales and the West Country that must have taken even the ever-optimistic Norman Edgar by surprise. Work commenced in February and was sufficiently advanced for flying operations to begin towards the end of May. The exact date that flying commenced is somewhat difficult to determine but an RAS Dragon 2 reportedly landed there on a proving flight on 23 May, prior to the commencement of RAS summer operations which included Weston in the timetable from 25 May. The management of the aerodrome was vested in Western Airways who moved their headquarters to Weston in June while maintaining a base at Bristol to handle the Bristol-Cardiff traffic.

Both companies found the public response to Cardiff-Weston services literally overwhelming and so great was the demand that Western Airways felt obliged to publish an apology to the many disappointed would-be passengers who could not be accommodated on the weekend of 30-31 May.

The reasons for the popularity of the route were manifold. Both places were popular destinations, Cardiff as a shopping centre for West Country folk and Weston as a holiday resort and daytrip centre for the Welsh, especially on Sundays when local licensing laws compelled the bibulous section of the community to seek solace either in England or afloat on Bristol Channel paddle steamers. Both aerodromes were close to the centres of population and the thirteen-mile distance could be traversed in less than ten minutes, cutting hours off the road and rail journeys and allowing a very competitive fare structure. There can, in fact, have been few occasions in air transport history when an airline has been able to operate profitably when charging less than the third class rail fare but Western Airways did, charging 6s 6d single and 9s 6d return, as opposed to 8s and 11s 2d on the hourly train service.

RAS too profited greatly from the route. Initially from 25 May the Cardiff-based Dragon left at 10.25 a.m. for Weston and Bristol with connections to the Liverpool-Shoreham service. It then retraced its path to Cardiff in readiness for a 11.30 a.m. departure to Plymouth with a request stop at Haldon, the proprietors of Denbury having gone out of business. Having arrived back at Cardiff at 5.25 p.m., it then repeated the morning's Weston-Bristol and return sectors.

Between 5 July and 6 September RAS introduced a Sunday 'Flying Day Out' – an excursion service leaving Cardiff at 9.45 a.m. and routing via Weston, Bristol, Southampton, the Isle of Wight, to Brighton where it arrived at 11.45 a.m. The returning aeroplane departed Brighton at 5.40 p.m. and arrived back at Cardiff at 7.40 p.m. Between 22 August and the closure of operations on 12 September, RAS entered into direct competition with Western Airways mounting an hourly Cardiff-Weston service, with the first departure at 10.25 a.m. and the last arrival at 8.15 p.m.

As the holiday season progressed, so activity between Cardiff and Weston grew more frenetic by the day. Figures released by Western Airways for all its services, which by then included a Weston-Birmingham route showed 2,496 passengers carried in June, 3,149 in July and over 5,000 in August, most of whom travelled Weston-Cardiff. In fact the company carried more passengers in the first two weeks of August than in the whole of 1935!

During peak periods it would appear that the company abandoned all pretence of schedule keeping, its fleet of Dragons simply criss-crossing the Channel as often as they possibly could. As previously, Western Airways continued to operate throughout the winter to both Bristol and Weston, the Weston schedule being reduced to five daily return services except for the Christmas period when demand was such that a half hourly schedule was introduced, often flown by three aeroplanes at a time.

Figures released at the end of the year revealed that in the first six months of operation Weston-super-Mare Aerodrome had handled 18,738 passengers to all destinations while Cardiff's throughput was close on 20,000 for the year.

In other parts of the county too, people were able to look back on 1936 as a year of achievement.

At Porthcawl, the newly established Pine's Airways had enjoyed a successful first season having carried several thousand passengers on joy rides.

The company's founder, Mr G.S. Pine, a local garage proprietor, who had learned to fly with the Cardiff Aeroplane Club in 1934, acquired a D.H.83 Fox Moth G-ACEX in April 1936 with which he mounted a joy riding and charter operation charging from 2s 6d for a short circuit to £2 for scenic flights along the South Wales coast to Cardiff or Mumbles. Also, because aircraft engaged in public transport were subject to a daily inspection by a licensed engineer, the ritual positioning flight to and from Pengam departing at 9.00 a.m. became, in effect, a scheduled service at a price of £1 per head until Mr Pine overcame the problem by becoming a licensed engineer in March 1938.

From 1938 onward the company also undertook some army co-operation flying acting as a target for searchlight or gunlaying practice or as 'enemy' aircraft making mock attacks on Territorial Army units during their summer camps at Porthcawl. A second Fox Moth G-ABVK was acquired in February 1939 along with a second pilot. The two aeroplanes became in fact as much a part of the seaside scene as the Coney Beach funfair

In August Capt. C.D. Godfrey's dream became reality when ninety acres of the Jersey Marine site at Swansea received Air Ministry approval for public transport operations. The aerodrome had in fact been used by a number of private fliers that year, particularly in May, by visitors to the Bath and West Agricultural Show staged in nearby Neath.

The last newsworthy event of the year in the west of the county was a forced landing, skillfully executed by George Pine alongside the main road between Margam and the Kenfig Pool on 21 December following an engine failure.

Despite the expenditure of £5,561 on drainage work at Pengam waterlogging was proving to be a problem still, resulting in several periods of closure in March and April 1937 with the inevitable cancellation of services. Even when the airport was open one observer described arriving aeroplanes as looking as if they were descending a water chute.

Poster advertising Pine's Airways.
(Porthcawl Museum)

D.H.83 Fox Moth of Pine's Airways after its accident on 6 June 1937. (Porthcawl Museum)

Normality was restored towards the end of April when Western Airways reverted to their summer schedules as per the previous year, their fleet augmented from May onwards by the acquisition of a D.H.89 Dragon Rapide, G-ADDD previously the property of the recently abdicated King Edward VIII. Despite an increase in fares to 8*s* single and 12*s* return, attributed to a rise in fuel prices, passenger numbers continued to grow reaching a peak on Bank Holiday Monday, 2 August, when 310 people made the channel crossing. Even so, the company found the capacity to undertake a charter from Cardiff to London's Heston Aerodrome between 8 and 9 May when two aeroplanes conveyed Rugby League supporters to the cup final.

The RAS summer season ran from 10 May to 25 September, the timetable being similar to the previous year except for the omission of Weston-super-Mare from the Cardiff-Bristol-Cardiff services and the inclusion, from its opening on 1 June of the Straight Corporation's aerodrome at Exeter, by request only, on the Cardiff-Plymouth route.

Except for two relatively minor accidents the year was unremarkable. On 6 June George Pine's Fox Moth struck a low wall while attempting to take off from Porthcawl, sustaining damage to the propeller, undercarriage and the port lower wing, without injury to Pine or his four passengers. A similar fate befell a Percival Vega Gull of Air Hire Ltd, of Heston at Jersey Marine on 7 October, again with no injury to the pilot, Mr R.H. Barlow, and his two passengers.

Despite the existence of Jersey Marine Aerodrome, it appears that Swansea Sands were still favoured as a landing ground by some, if newspaper reports of the landing of an undisclosed type of aeroplane there on 4 March, whose occupants successfully retrieved their younger brother who was in the process of running away to sea, are to be believed.

The period of stability and steady growth that characterised the internal air transport industry in the south and west of England and South Wales during the preceding six years, ended abruptly at the beginning of 1938, brought about by a number of takeovers and mergers

D.H.83 Fox Moth of Pine's Airways at Porthcawl. (Porthcawl Museum)

Frank Keast of Pine's Airways. (Porthcawl Museum)

accompanied by damaging competition both locally and elsewhere that led ultimately to Government intervention.

In February 1938 it was announced that the Straight Corporation, which had apparently taken a financial interest in Western Airways the previous year, had acquired control of the company. Founded in 1934 by the then twenty-one-year-old wealthy American-born, natu-ralised British racing motorist, aviator and entrepreneur, Whitney Willard Straight, the organisation's many constituent companies controlled aerodromes and flying clubs at Ramsgate, Ipswich, Exeter, Haldon, Plymouth and Inverness and by the outbreak of war had grown into a conglomerate of twenty-one separate companies. Flt Lt W.E. Knowlden of the Straight Corporation assumed the position of operations manager and manager of Weston-super-Mare Aerodrome while Norman Edgar remained as commercial director, although later in the year his name was dropped from the company's title at the same time as Western Air Transport Ltd was renamed Straightaway Ltd. Except for the fleet being resprayed in the straight Corporation's colours of metallic grey with red and white striped rudders and a reduction of fares on the Weston-Cardiff route to their original 6s 6d single, 9s 6d return, the takeover had little effect on the travelling public.

A more sinister event from the viewpoint of both Western Airways and RAS was the arrival at Pengam on 21 February of a D.H.89 Dragon Rapide on the inaugural flight of Channel Air Ferries Brighton (Shoreham)-Isle of Wight (Bembridge)-Bournemouth-Bristol-Cardiff services. Channel Air Ferries Ltd was a subsidiary of Olley Air Service Ltd, founded by the same Capt. G.P. Olley who had flown the GWR services in 1933, which operated a number of services along the South Coast including, significantly, Plymouth-Penzance-Scilly. The service pre-empted RAS's summer schedules, which commenced on 23 May, by three months and in part duplicated the RAS north-south route which that year ran from Manchester to Brighton via Liverpool, Birmingham, Gloucester (Staverton) (on request), Bristol, Southampton and the Isle of Wight and also the Cardiff-Bristol return sec-tors that preceded and succeeded the daily Cardiff-Exeter-Plymouth service. It also, of course, provided even more competition to Western Airways on their Bristol-Cardiff service.

Activity at Cardiff that summer was more hectic than ever. Western Airways figures for the Easter period showed 500 passengers carried between Weston and Cardiff on Easter Sunday 17 April and 600 the following day. The Royal Show held at Pontcanna Fields from 4 July brought more interesting visitors in the form of sheep from Barnstaple aboard a Short Scion of Atlantic Coast Air Services and sixteen Jersey farmers aboard a D.H.86 of Jersey Airways. All RAS services were fully booked that week and the Weston-Cardiff ferry was operated at times in triplicate. Another unusual visitor which arrived on Monday 15 August was a Junkers Ju 52 of the German airline Lufthansa that flew in to evacuate two seriously injured German nationals.

Swansea joined the growing list of towns and cities surrounding the Bristol Channel to be served by an air service on Wednesday 27 July 1938 when, having taken over the lease of Jersey Marine Aerodrome, the Straight Corporation and Western Airways inaugurated a twice-daily service linking Swansea to Cardiff and Weston. The timing of the service, with a morning arrival at 9.55 a.m. followed by a departure at 10.00 a.m. and evening arrivals and departures at 7.55 p.m. and 8.00 p.m. popular with both arriving and departing businessmen, ensured its immediate success.

The inaugural flight, piloted by Flt Lt Knowlden, embarked various local dignitaries including Sir Arthur and Lady Whitten-Brown from the Swansea Bay Golf Club, which served as the terminal building and conveyed them to Weston for lunch as guests of Mr Whitney Straight who followed in his Percival Gull. Although intended to close for the winter on 19 September, the service proved sufficiently popular for a twice-weekly Monday and Friday service to be maintained throughout the winter months.

By the end of July the directors of RAS and Channel Air Ferries had recognised the futility of competition and embarked instead on a policy of co-operation by pooling their resources pending the setting up of a new company to serve their common interests. Consequently from 8 August the Bristol-Cardiff-Exeter-Plymouth service was operated on alternate days by RAS and Channel Air Ferries aeroplanes which continued on demand to Land's End with a connection to Scilly, until the service ended for the winter on 30 September.

The darkening autumn evenings brought about another innovation when both Weston and Cardiff Aerodromes having been approved for night flying, the former Royal Dragon Rapide, G-ADDD, of Western Airways piloted by Flt Lt Knowlden, with Whitney Straight and various dignitaries aboard, touched down at Pengam on Sunday 2 October 1938 having completed the first scheduled internal night service in the UK.

The service operated on demand but soon the old bogey of waterlogging at Pengam returned and the airport was closed on 30 November and seems to have been out of service for most of the time until the following March. Nevertheless on the whole 1938 was a year of considerable success, Western Airways alone having carried over 22,000 passengers into and out of Pengam.

In December, Whitney Straight approached Cardiff City Council with a view to taking over the lease of Pengam, building a hotel and starting a Straight Corporation-owned flying club there, in fact he registered a new company, Glamorgan Aero Club Ltd, with that end in mind, but his offer was met with a refusal.

The co-operation between RAS and Channel Air Ferries culminated on 5 December 1938 in the incorporation of Great Western & Southern Air Lines Ltd. The company, whose headquarters were at Brighton (Shoreham) Airport, was designed to serve the aviation interests of the GWR, the Southern Railway and those of Channel Air Ferries, the £100,000 investment being borne fifty per cent by British and Foreign Aviation Ltd, the holding company for Channel Air Ferries and Olley Air Service, and twenty-five per cent each by the two railway companies.

As only a few Channel Air Ferries routes were operated during the winter months the company continued to trade under that name until 24 March 1939 when all services were operated under the Great Western & Southern Air Lines banner.

During the summer of 1938, the Government, keen to encourage the progress of civil aviation while preventing the uneconomic competition that was beginning to develop in some areas, had established the Air Transport Licensing Authority, a body, as its name implied, charged with regulating by means of a licensing system, the allocation of routes to suitable operators and also controlling the frequency of operation. A further move, the grant of a small financial subsidy to holders of route licences, was planned to take effect from 1 January 1939.

The process of processing applications, holding public hearings and adjudicating on the

George Pine of Pine's Airways in front of D.H.83 Fox Moth at Porthcawl in 1939. (Porthcawl Museum)

numerous objections and counter objections took longer than anticipated but by the spring of 1939 a system of licensed air routes was in place throughout the UK.

As far as services affecting South Wales were concerned the outcome was as follows: Western Airways were licenced to operate: Weston-Cardiff, Bristol-Cardiff, Cardiff-Swansea, Weston-Bristol-Birmingham-Manchester, and Bristol-Swansea-Barnstaple-Newquay-Penzance; Great Western & Southern Air Lines received licences for the routes Liverpool-Manchester-Birmingham-Bristol-Ryde-Shoreham, Shoreham-Ryde-Bourne-mouth-Bristol-Cardiff, Bristol-Exeter-Plymouth-Penzance and Penzance-Scilly. Lundy and Atlantic Coast Airlines retained the right to fly from Barnstaple to Lundy but were deemed to be too small a company to be able to guarantee a regular service between Barnstaple and Cardiff and were not granted a licence to do so.

The period of inactivity at Cardiff, which obviously affected all destinations served from there, was broken at the beginning of March when Western Airways, frustrated, and, according to a letter from Flt Lt Knowlden, published in the *Western Mail*, angry at the City Council's inability to drain Pengam, commenced a restricted service of four daily flights to and from Wenvoe Aerodrome. It would appear that Weston was the only destination served until about 21 March when normal operations at Pengam were resumed.

By 5 April the company was advertising an hourly service to Weston departing on the hour between 9.00 a.m. and 6.00 p.m. and by 6 May a half-hourly service between 8.30 a.m. and 10.30 p.m. making the service the world's most frequent airline schedule. To cope with the demand a four-engined, sixteen-seat D.H.86B G-AETM was acquired to augment the fleet of three D.H.89 Dragon Rapides and five D.H.84 Dragons.

The summer season for both Western Airways and Great Western & Southern Airlines began in earnest on 8 May. From that date, in addition to the Weston-Cardiff services, Western Airways' timetable included five daily departures from Swansea to Bristol via Cardiff leaving Swansea at 9.20 a.m., 12.00 p.m., 4.20 p.m., 6.20 p.m. and 8.20 p.m. and Cardiff at 9.45 a.m., 12.25 p.m., 4.45 p.m., 6.45 p.m. and 8.45 p.m., the first three of which connected at Bristol with the company's services to Birmingham and Manchester. There were five flights in the opposite direction originating from Bristol and departing Cardiff at 8.50 a.m., 11.30 a.m., 2.50 p.m., 5.50 p.m. and 7.50 p.m., two of which, the 8.50 a.m. and 5.50 p.m., continued to Barnstaple, the Swansea-Barnstaple flight time of twenty-five minutes comparing favourably with the nine hours taken by train! The 11.30 a.m. departure continued beyond Barnstaple to Newquay and Penzance, also known as Lands End (St. Just).

The formula of high frequency, short turnaround times and low fares which was the significant feature of Western Airways operation guaranteed continuing success. Over the five days of Whitsun 1939, 1,843 passengers were carried on the company's scheduled services and on Bank Holiday Monday, 7 August, over 1,000 on flights to and from Cardiff alone.

The Great Western & Southern Air Lines services were much the same as those operated by RAS and Channel Air Ferries in 1938 with the exception of the extension of the Plymouth route to Penzance in order to connect with services to Scilly. Sadly what had become a thriving industry, particularly in South Wales and the West Country was overwhelmed by world events and the 1939 summer season was somewhat shorter than planned.

Having chronicled the successes of various operators, I feel it necessary, as a matter of historical record, to refer to the failure of another, namely Cambrian Air Services. In a letter, a copy of which, dated only 1939, is still in existence, the chairman, Mr S.K. Davies pointed out to his fellow directors that the company's sole assets were a shareholding in Western Airways valued at £70 and debtors. Mr Davies went on to say 'I see nothing for the future of this company but I might have some use for the name', and offered to purchase their shareholding for a small sum, concluding 'otherwise I do not see any particular object in keeping it alive.' Apparently his offer was rejected and, although the company lay dormant for a further seven years, Mr Davies' predictions proved incorrect, with Cambrian Air Services, later renamed Cambrian Airways, becoming a major player in post-war Welsh aviation.

In conclusion it is appropriate to pay tribute to those men of vision who laid the foundations of the events described and those men of action – ground staff, engineers and, particularly, pilots – who built on them. I feel that only a pilot can fully appreciate the skill and dedication of those who spent long hours flying those small, ill-equipped aeroplanes with a paucity of en route and terminal navigation aids in all weathers, into and out of small, ill-equipped, ill-lit, often waterlogged, grass aerodromes with such safety and regularity. They were men apart.

18
Military Aviation

The political events that culminated in the outbreak of the Second World War are too well known to warrant much repetition. Suffice it to say that Adolf Hitler's rise to power in 1933 dispelled all hopes of a lasting world peace and, in Britain, led to a re-appraisal of the nation's defence strategy. In the case of the RAF, which at that time was responsible for all military aviation, it became apparent that although the service was the subject of an ongoing expansion plan, initiated in 1923 and still incomplete, its equipment was woefully lacking in both quality and quantity.

As a consequence, between 1934 and 1939 the RAF was subjected to no less than eight further expansion plans which for practical purposes may be regarded as one. The plans called not only for an enormous increase in the RAF's overall strength but also for its re-equipment with a new generation of aircraft types, monoplanes instead of the outmoded biplanes, with which all front line units were then equipped.

Such an expansion could not, of course, be accomplished without an extensive programme of recruitment, training, reorganisation and redeployment. For ease of administration the service was organised into commands, each responsible for its own sphere of operations. Bomber, Fighter, Coastal and Training Commands were established in 1936 followed by Maintenance Command in 1938 and Reserve Command in 1939. The overall strategy dictated that bomber and fighter squadrons should be redeployed from the south to the east of the country to face the potential aggressor, coastal squadrons be maintained at locations around the coasts to protect major sea lanes leaving training and maintenance units in the west where they would be safe from air attack. It must be remembered that at the time the plans were drawn up the western part of the country was virtually out of range of bombers based in Germany and it was only after the fall of France that Luftwaffe bombers and fighters were able to operate with ease over most of Britain.

Beside the regular service, provision was made to expand the Auxiliary Air Force and to establish a Royal Air Force Volunteer Reserve, an organisation which trained no less than 10,217 aircrew volunteers by September 1939. Other volunteers provided the personnel to man ground-based defences in the form of anti-aircraft batteries of the Territorial Army and balloon barrage squadrons of the Auxiliary Air Force.

Needless to say such an expansion brought about a requirement for many additional service aerodromes. Their construction, which commenced in the mid-1930s and continued at an ever increasing pace for almost a decade, left few areas of the United Kingdom unaffected and changed the British landscape for ever.

With the Air Ministry's general strategy public knowledge, speculation began to arise in South Wales as elsewhere as to the RAF's potential involvement with the area. Various public figures motivated by ideas as diverse as the air defence of the South Wales ports and their industrial hinterland, unemployment relief or personal pecuniary gain, began to ask questions and to lobby the Air Ministry. The Ministry for its part maintained an extraordinary policy

Hawker Hectors of 614 Squadron in formation. (Edwin Chamberlain)

of silence or sometimes outright denial that only served to fuel rumours, most of which proved to be remarkably accurate.

For instance, Ministry spokesmen repeatedly denied all knowledge of plans to construct an aerodrome at Stormy Down, near Porthcawl, despite the fact that it was common knowledge locally that the site had been surveyed as early as September 1934 and connected to mains water in November 1936. They also categorically stated that no units of the Auxiliary Air Force would be raised in Wales and in August 1935, when rejecting one of several tenders by Mr R.H. Thomas to establish an Elementary and Reserve Flying School in the district, used the words 'the building of an air depot in South Wales does not fall in with the tactical defence plan of the British Isles.'

However, speculation continued throughout the spring and summer of 1936 fuelled by a somewhat enigmatic statement made at the end of February by the former Prime Minister Ramsey MacDonald which coincided with claims by local residents that an air marshal and several other men had been seen in the vicinity of Eglwys Brewis in the Vale of Glamorgan. In the event the only significant flying of a military nature that year was from Pengam during August by a civil Short Scion on an army co-operation contract in support of the guns and searchlights of Territorial Army detachments in camp at Porthcawl.

It was not until the autumn of 1936 that the Air Ministry began to reveal its plans, the enormity of which must have surprised even the most imaginative of speculators. Within the space of a few months it was announced that not only would one of four new Auxiliary Air Force squadrons be based at a considerably enlarged Pengam Aerodrome but also that the entire

Hawker Hectors of 614 Squadron in formation over Cardiff city centre. (Edwin Chamberlain)

parish of Eglwys Brewis along with other surrounding land, comprising West Orchard, Broadway and Fisher's Bridge Farms plus seventy acres of Glamorgan County Council small-holdings, some 895 acres in all, had been acquired at a cost of £58,300 for the purpose of constructing the largest RAF station in the country, the total cost of the project being estimated at £820,000. The ground was vacated by 31 December 1936 and the main contractor, Messrs Demolition & Construction Ltd, commenced clearance work on the site shortly afterwards. In the course of the following eighteen months a labour force which at its peak numbered 2,000 men, completed what, in deference to those unable to get to grips with Welsh pronunciation, became known as RAF St Athan, after the village situated to the east of its boundary.

The completed station consisted in effect of two distinct and separate areas, East Camp and West Camp sharing a common grass aerodrome, its intended role being as a multi-purpose, non-operational airfield catering for storage and maintenance as well as both technical and flying training. Except for the wartime addition of hard runways and the post-war replacement of East Camp's wooden hutted accommodation with permanent brick billet blocks, the station and its roles has changed little since.

The promised Auxiliary Air Force Squadron No.614 (County of Glamorgan) officially formed at Pengam on 1 June 1937 when its first adjutant, Flt Lt P. Morgan-Smith opened an office at the airport. The Auxiliary Air Force, the prefix Royal was not bestowed until 1947, was founded in 1925 under the provisions of the Auxiliary Air Force and Air Force Reserve Act of 1924. The act provided for the raising of front line squadrons, manned in the main by part-time volunteers recruited on a territorial basis and administered by local Territorial

Army and Air Force Associations. Initially those squadrons fell into two differing categories, Special Reserve squadrons, distinguished by their numbers in the 500 series, 501 Squadron for example, which were effectively regular squadrons based in a particular area but which admitted a percentage of Auxiliary Air Force personnel, and Auxiliary squadrons proper numbered in the 600 range. However by 1936 all sixteen squadrons then extant had achieved full Auxiliary Air Force status.

Auxiliary squadrons had, of necessity, a nucleus of regular RAF personnel. They included the adjutant and assistant adjutant, both of whom doubled as flying instructors, the stores officer and a substantial number of NCOs and airmen who, besides being responsible for the day-to-day running of the squadron, also served as instructional staff. However, the commanding officer, all other aircrew and the majority of ground staff were auxiliaries.

The major difference between auxiliary squadrons and their regular counterparts was that, with the exception of pilots, who were required to hold civil A or B licences prior to enrolment, all auxiliary squadron members were trained from scratch and in house. Pilot candidates who were deemed to be otherwise suitable but did not hold appropriate licences could be provisionally enrolled pending obtaining a licence, the cost of training being repaid by the Air Ministry. Further basic and advanced flying training was then provided by the squadron.

The major difference between 614 Squadron and previous auxiliary squadrons was its role – army co-operation, as opposed to the fighter or bomber roles of previous units. That in turn meant that in common with regular army co-operations squadrons there was a requirement for all pilots to be of commissioned rank.

The build up of the squadron continued for the remainder of the year. Effective from 8 June, former R.F.C. captain, prominent South Wales businessman and Cardiff Aeroplane Club director, Richard Cadman, was granted a commission with the rank of squadron leader and appointed to command. On 15 June the first aeroplanes, two Avro Tutor basic trainers, arrived and were temporarily accommodated in the club hangar. An advance party of the squadron's regular personnel arrived at the same time. Flying training for the first recruits appears to have commenced at the beginning of August and continued for the rest of the year.

The advent of 614 Squadron was not attended with feelings of unconfined joy in all quarters particularly when the extent of the Air Ministry's plans for the airport became known. In order to extend the landing area the holders of some 700 council allotments adjoining the northern and western boundaries were given notice to quit by September 1937. Work then began on the construction of hangars, workshops, offices, messing and sleeping quarters at the north east corner of the airfield adjacent to the original Whitaker Road entrance which became the entrance to the military section of the airfield. A new civil entrance was constructed in Tweedsmuir Road adjacent to its junction with Taymuir Road and the Cardiff Aeroplane Club accommodation and hangar was relocated to the north east corner. The total estimated expenditure was £105,000. Concern was voiced that the military operations would have an adverse, if not dangerous, effect on civil flying and that it would have been more appropriate to have based the squadron at St Athan. However, with the benefit of hindsight, it is apparent that the militarisation of Pengam formed part of a much longer-term plan that was only revealed after the outbreak of hostilities.

Public disapproval was also expressed when, in November 1937, the long-expected announcement of the building of an RAF station at Stormy Down was made, particularly when the nature of the station's intended role, armament training, became known. Nevertheless Messrs Garrard & Sons, the main contractors, commenced work in March 1938. The cost of the project was initially estimated at £180,000 but seems to have gradually escalated to some £280,000 by the time the contract was completed.

It is worth mentioning in passing that a significant adjunct to the airfield building programme was a corresponding programme of council house building in neighbouring towns intended to accommodate the planned influx of civilian employees of the Air Ministry, particularly to St Athan. In the event, however, the outbreak of war disrupted the original plans and resulted in relatively few houses being used for their intended purpose.

The 614 Squadron training programme continued apace throughout 1938, the high point being the squadron's first annual training camp held at RAF Hawkinge, Kent, between 2 and 9 July. A Hawker Hart Trainer and two Hawker Hind Trainers were added to the squadron's inventory for advanced training of pilots prior to their conversion to the squadron's front line type, the Hawker Hector.

The conversion of pilots to the Hector was not without incident. On 3 April K9784 was damaged beyond repair and its pilot, Plt-Off. Richard Rhys, slightly injured in a landing accident at Pengam. A similar fate befell K8109 on 4 June while K9728 was damaged in a forced landing due to inclement weather at Oakenholt Farm, Flint, on 7 September.

Empire Air Day, 28 May, was for the first time chosen as the occasion for Cardiff's annual air display. Previous Empire Air Days, always held at the end of May, had passed virtually unnoticed due to the fact that although Pengam and Wenvoe Aerodromes had usually opened their gates to the public, no entertainment had been provided beyond the odd impromptu aerobatic display and at Pengam in 1936 a flypast by aeroplanes of 501 Squadron. In fact in 1937 due to the proximity of the Coronation Air Rally there had been no Empire Air Day celebrations at all.

Times, however, were changing and so was Empire Air Day. Originally conceived as a national celebration of flight in general, it had by 1938 taken on a more sinister role as a celebration of the RAF's increasing strength. The celebrations included not only flying displays at RAF stations and other venues throughout the country on the day itself but also during the preceding week, flypasts over major centres of population by large formations of military aircraft. For instance, in the evening of Monday 23 May a formation of forty-two aircraft, mostly Hawker Hind light bombers, appeared over Cardiff while at various times the following day three further formations flew along the South Wales coast. The first consisted of twelve Bristol Blenheim bombers, the second a mixed formation of 45 Fairey Battle bombers and 27 Hawker Hinds and the third twelve Avro Anson maritime reconnaissance aeroplanes.

On the Saturday itself, despite traffic chaos caused by the new airport entrance, a record crowd assembled at Pengam to view a static display of military aeroplanes and equipment and witness a flying display that included aerobatics and formation flying by Hawker Harts, a Hawker Fury fighter, Fairey Battle and Handley Page Heyford bombers and a display of army co-operation flying by Hawker Hectors. The only civil participation being joy riding by aeroplanes of Western Airways Ltd, a far cry from the garden party atmosphere of previous years.

As had become usual, August was a period of intense Territorial Army activity with many thousands of troops encamped at Porthcawl and at Porthkerry near Barry and, as previously, Pines Airways provided 'enemy' aircraft to 'attack' both the Porthcawl camp and motor transport convoys.

The commanding officer of 614 Squadron, Sqdn Ldr Richard Cadman, and some of his pilots in front of a Hawker Hector at Pengam Moors, c.1938. (Edwin Chamberlain)

RAF St Athan became operational under the command of Group Capt. E. Brownsdon-Rice on 1 September 1938 when an advance party of twenty-five airmen arrived at East Camp to prepare for the arrival, in the course of the following seven weeks, of a further 1,000 staff and trainees of No.4 School of Technical Training.

The waterlogging of Pengam affected 614 Squadron's activities in just the same way as everybody else's. Following a mock attack on Cardiff for the benefit of the Territorial Army at the end of October 1938 the squadron remained grounded until the beginning of March 1939.

However, another Auxiliary Air Force unit formed at Cardiff during that period. No.935 (County of Glamorgan) Balloon Barrage, one of many such units formed at that time, under the command of Sqn Ldr E.J.S.L. Brooke MC, occupied temporary headquarters at Windsor Slipway at the bottom of South Clive Street. The unit commenced recruiting on 31 January 1939. Cardiff Corporation, realising that compulsory purchase was the only alternative, agreed to sell a plot of land adjacent to Caerau Lane, Ely, then in use as allotments (now the site of the Western Leisure Centre) to the Air Ministry as a permanent base for the unit. Known as RAF Llandaff, presumably to avoid confusion with Ely, Cambridgeshire, the station, complete with two balloon hangars, opened in August 1939.

In order to stimulate interest and aid recruiting, a barrage balloon, illuminated at night by searchlights, was flown from 31 March to 1 April from Cathays Park during which period a recruiting film 'Man the Barrage' was shown at the Empire Theatre. It was also the occasion for the embryo unit's first inspection by Air Vice Marshal O.T. Boyd, Air Officer Commanding Balloon Command, who inspected the Windsor Slipway and the Ely site.

Engine run on Hawker Hector of 614 Squadron at Pengam Moors. Note the construction work in progress in the background. (Edwin Chamberlain)

Empire Air Day celebrations commenced on 8 May 1939 when a formation of fifty-four Fairey Battles flew from the east along the coast as far as St Athan before retracing their route. On 13 May no fewer than seventy-two battles on a route Abingdon-Cirencester-Newport-Cardiff-Barry-Bristol-Abingdon must have made an impressive sight and sound in the South Wales skies.

On Saturday 20 May over 15,000 visitors attended the display at Pengam. It opened and closed with a flypast by a Short Sunderland flying boat from RAF Pembroke Dock. Other types present included a North American Harvard trainer, the first to be seen (and heard) in the district. Miles Magister, Anson, Battles and nine Hectors and two Tutors of 614 Squadron were present. The squadron was virtually fully operational by that time and played a major part in the display. Shortly afterwards it commenced to re-equip with Westland Lysander aircraft some of which had arrived by the time the squadron left for its annual camp at Hawkinge in July.

Meanwhile, further to the west, rapid developments had taken place during the year. On 7 February 1939 at St Athan No.9 Aircraft Storage Unit which had formed, on paper at least, at the end of 1938 was redesignated No.19 Maintenance Unit, a predominantly civilian-manned unit. The term maintenance unit, like so much RAF terminology can be somewhat misleading to the uninitiated, having been applied to units dealing with items as diverse as clothing and armaments. No.19 MU was an aircraft storage unit. Such units were tasked with receiving aircraft either from the manufacturer or on return from operational units, maintaining, modifying and storing them prior to issuing or re-issuing them into service. They were also responsible for dismantling time-expired machines.

Officers of 614 Squadron in front of a Hawker Hector at Pengam Moors, c.1938. (Edwin Chamberlain)

Later, on 1 July, a second MU No.32, manned by service personnel, came into being but did not become fully operational until October. Both MUs were centred on West Camp with dispersal sites around the airfield perimeter. As the year progressed aerial activity over the Vale of Glamorgan increased dramatically as aircraft arrived, departed and flew on air-test from St Athan. Soon Avro Ansons, Fairey Battles, Bristol Blenheims, Handley Page Hampdens, Westland Lysanders and De Havilland Tiger Moths became familiar sights in the local skies.

1 July 1939 also saw the arrival at St Athan from Andover of No.11 (Fighter) Group Pool equipped with Fairey Battles and Hawker Hurricanes. Another case of curious RAF nomenclature, Group Pools came into existence at the beginning of 1939 in order to relieve front line squadrons of the task of converting newly qualified pilots onto their operational aircraft types. They later evolved into and were more appropriately titled Operational Training Units. No.11 Group Pool was tasked with converting pilots onto the Hawker Hurricane fighter which was to play such a major role in the Battle of Britain. The course consisted of dual instruction in handling the Rolls-Royce Merlin engine in the Fairey Battle before proceeding to the single-seat Merlin-engined Hurricane I.

The aerodrome at Stormy Down opened officially on 1 June 1939 under the command of Wg Cdr J.C.P. Wood, who handed over to Wing Commandeer T.O. Cloughstoun the following week. The station was variously known as RAF Porthcawl, which caused confusion with nearby Lock's Common and RAF Newton Down, which caused confusion with RAF Newton, Nottinghamshire, before finally being renamed RAF Stormy Down, the name by which it is best remembered, in November 1940.

Designated No.9 Armament Training Station it was a much smaller station than St Athan with an establishment of some 200 Officers, NCOs and Airmen.

Armament Training Stations were established in suitable coastal locations to provide armament training for units, mostly Flying Training Schools, who were unable for safety reasons to undertake such activities at their home bases. They consisted of an aerodrome and adjacent ranges where high and low level bombing and air to air and air to ground gunnery training could be safely undertaken. Trainees, along with their instructors and aeroplanes, were normally detached to such establishments for periods of up to three weeks during their advanced training. The only resident aircraft were normally target tugs.

In the case of Newton Down a bombing and air to ground gunnery range was established along the beach on the Port Talbot side of the Kenfig River with further targets located off shore in the vicinity of Sker. In addition an air to air firing area was established between the coast and a line joining Nash Point and Tusker Rock. Such activities must have proved somewhat of a problem to Western Airways' Cardiff-Swansea operations. In order to service the offshore targets and to provide range safety boats a Marine Craft Unit was established in Porthcawl Harbour.

Target towing was carried out by five Hawker Henley III aeroplanes, later increased to seven, which along with a single Miles Magister of the station flight were the only aircraft permanently based at the station prior to the outbreak of hostilities.

The station was visited on 20 June by Air Marshal Sir Charles Burnett, Air Officer Commanding RAF Training Command who flew in on a tour of inspection. Operations commenced on 31 July with the arrival of a detachment of Airspeed Oxfords from No.5 Flying Training School RAF Sealand near Chester. They remained until 25 August. They were followed by a second detachment of Oxfords from No.3 FTS RAF South Cerney, Gloucestershire, which arrived on 29 August and were still in situ when war broke out.

The upsurge in military aviation activity during the summer of 1939 was not achieved without incident.

On the evening of 6 July an Avro Anson of 217 Squadron, Coastal Command, based at RAF Tangmere, Sussex, piloted by the squadron's commanding officer, Wg Cdr A.P. Revington was forced to land on the beach at Sker near Porthcawl due to a technical problem. Revington and his crew were unharmed but the aeroplane suffered damage to both propellers and, worse still, became bogged down in the wet sand. There ensued a desperate race against time and tide to free the machine and drag it above the high water mark.

The combined efforts of the crew, Mr Evan Evans of Sker Farm, a posse of his farm workers and a team of draught horses proved fruitless and it was not until they were augmented by a team of some sixty officers and men from Newton Down that the aeroplane was finally dragged to safety and picketed under guard for the night. It was subsequently dismantled and removed by road by a working party from No.4 School of Technical Training, St Athan, despite a bizarre attempt by Capt. A.M. Talbot-Fletcher of the Margam Estate to claim ownership under the law relating to flotsam which, unhappily for him, did not apply to Crown property.

A somewhat more serious accident occurred at Pengam in the evening of 3 August when Ft Lt Robert Lister, 614 Squadron's adjutant, and Pt-Off. Eric Latham apparently experienced an engine failure shortly after taking off in Hawker Hind Trainer L7239. In the course of the ensuing return to earth the aeroplane overran the landing ground and came to rest inverted in a ditch on the eastern boundary of the aerodrome. When extricated from the wreckage Ft Lt Lister was found to have received back injuries necessitating a spell in hospital. Pt-Off. Latham's injuries were of a less serious nature.

More fortunate was Sgt W.A. Doherty to whom on 15 August fell the dubious distinction of having the first accident at Newton Down. On returning from a target towing sortie his Hawker Henley overran the runway and terminated its flight in the hedge. Doherty was unhurt.

By September 1939, having started from scratch only two years and eight months previously, the Air Ministry had constructed three aerodromes in the county, one of them of enormous proportions, deployed several thousand personnel and close on 300 aircraft. It was an enormous achievement.

19
Epilogue

At daybreak on 1 September 1939 Germany, having previously made a number of territorial gains albeit with the acquiescence of the local populations, if not the international community, finally overstepped the mark and invaded Poland. As a result both France and Great Britain, who had guaranteed Poland's independence, were committed to war. There ensued a short period of futile diplomatic activity which both countries utilised to mobilise their armed forces before war was finally declared on 3 September.

In Britain it was widely expected that following the declaration of war eastern England would be subjected to immediate aerial bombardment and consequently measures were taken to minimise its effect. Besides the implementation of air raid precautions and the evacuation of school children from major centres of population, restrictions were placed on the movement of civil aircraft and a large scale redeployment of aircraft both civil and military commenced.

Initially civil aircraft were prohibited from flying over large areas of eastern Britain, and elsewhere, with the exception of takeoff and landing, restricted to the narrow band of airspace between 1,000ft and 3,000ft. The restrictions led to the cancellation of many internal air services including all serving South Wales with the exception of the Weston-Cardiff service of Western Airways.

The declaration of war on Sunday 3 September was the signal for the implementation of numerous carefully prepared plans including the withdrawal of large numbers of non-combatant aircraft to the safety of the west and the movement of some operational aircraft in the opposite direction. At the same time, club, sporting and non-essential commercial aviation was prohibited.

Within a very short time the nature of aerial activity in Glamorgan underwent a marked change. Jersey Marine and Wenvoe aerodromes closed, Pine's Airways ceased operating as did Cardiff Aeroplane Club and the privately owned aeroplanes based at Pengam. The Weston-Cardiff service ceased although it recommenced at a later date and 614 Squadron departed its birthplace for its designated war station at RAF Odiham, Hampshire.

Pengam, however, did not close for the Government had significant plans for its future, the first of which was as a base for aircraft of the newly formed National Air Communications organisation (NAC).

NAC, a department of the Air Ministry with headquarters at Bristol, came into being on 1 September 1939, tasked with co-ordinating the operation of civil aircraft on essential war work. One of the conditions attached to the recently introduced airline subsidy scheme required recipients to make their aircraft available to the Government in time of national emergency. As a consequence some 200 assorted civil aircraft came under NAC's control, most of which were withdrawn to safe bases in the west

Pengam became the designated war station for all aircraft owned or operated by Mrs Victor Bruce's Air Dispatch Ltd, some twenty-three in all, and also the fifteen-strong fleet of

Portsmouth Southsea & Isle of Wight Aviation Ltd. Most, if not all, the aircraft of both companies arrived on 3 September.

St Athan and Newton Down Aerodromes were placed on a war footing on 2 September. At St Athan preparations were made to receive the personnel and over fifty Avro Anson aircraft of No.1 School of Air Navigation which flew in on 4 September. Although the aircraft of No.3 FTS stayed at Newton Down until the course was completed, the station itself was re-designated No.7 Air Observers School with effect from 1 September. On 3 September the station received ten Westland Wallaces and five Hawker Henleys which had been on the strength of No.1 Air Observers School, North Coates, Lincolnshire – that unit having withdrawn to the relative safety of Penrhos and merged with No.9 AOS the previous day.

So the scene was set for war. The century had been punctuated again and what happened next is another story.

Index

Airships

Balloons

Personalities